The Malvern Hills
An ancient landscape

The Malvern Hills
An ancient landscape

Mark Bowden

with contributions by David Field and Helen Winton

ENGLISH HERITAGE

Published by English Heritage, 23 Savile Row, London W1S 2ET
www.english-heritage.org.uk

English Heritage is the Government's statutory adviser on all aspects of the historic
environment.

First published 2005

ISBN 1 873592 82 5

Product Code 50901

British Library Cataloguing in Publication Data
A CIP catalogue record for this book is available from the British Library.

The National Monuments Record is the public archive of English Heritage. For more
information, contact NMR Enquiry and Research Services, National Monuments
Record Centre, Kemble Drive, Swindon SN2 2GZ; telephone (01793) 414600.

Application for the reproduction of images should be made to the National
Monuments Record.

Edited and brought to publication by David M Jones, Publishing, English Heritage,
Kemble Drive, Swindon SN2 2GZ.

Proofread by Diana Smith
Cover design and page layout by Mark Simmons
Indexed by the author
Printed by Snoeck-Ducaju & Zoon, Ghent

Contents

Illustrations

Except where specified, all drawings are by Deborah Cunliffe, all aerial photographs by Damian Grady and all ground photographs by James O Davies.

English Heritage thanks the Society of Antiquaries of London for permission to reproduce H H Lines' drawing of British Camp and the Woolhope Naturalists Field Club for permission to reproduce Chris Musson's aerial photograph of Ledbury.

Acknowledgements

The following members of English Heritage staff took part in this Project: field investigation – Mark Bowden, Graham Brown, David Field and Nicky Smith; aerial reconnaissance and photography – Damian Grady; aerial transcription – Helen Winton and Fiona Small; ground photography – James O Davies; illustration – Deborah Cunliffe. Woodland survey was carried out by Tim Hoverd of Herefordshire Archaeology, Tim Grubb and Karen Derham of Gloucestershire CC Archaeology Service, and Adam Mindykowski and Jez Bretherton of Worcestershire CC Archaeological Service, assisted by Nicky Gooch, Michael McCurdy and Don Williams. Documentary research was undertaken by Valerie Goodbury. The EH field team was assisted by students on placement at various times – Simon Jeffrey, Jill Hind, Danielle Wootton and Alys Spillman – and by one of the first EPPIC placements, John Lord.

The Project was managed by a steering group consisting of David Hancock and subsequently Amanda McCleery (AONB Officers), David Armitage (AONB Project Officer), Mark Bowden (EH), Tim Grubb (Gloucestershire), Dr Keith Ray and Tim Hoverd (Herefordshire), and Malcolm Atkin and Jez Bretherton (Worcestershire). Overall management for EH was by Paul Everson, enthusiastically supported at the outset by Humphrey Welfare, then Director of Survey within the RCHME.

During the preparation of this book Derek Hurst and Deborah Overton of Worcestershire Archaeological Service, and Melissa Seddon of Herefordshire Archaeology supplied much valuable information. Professor Richard Bradley, Dr Mike Parker Pearson, Charlotte Stamper and Dr Paul Stamper kindly commented on parts of the draft text. The preparation of the book also benefitted from discussions with Graham Brown, Paul Everson, David Field, Nicky Smith and Helen Winton.

English Heritage wishes to thank the following for their help: Roger Clark, Lynn Clearwaters, Simon Foster, James Harvey-Bathurst, David Heaver, Joe Hillaby, Graeme Kirkham, Tom Moore and Amanda Simons.

English Heritage would also like to thank Malvern Hills AONB Partnership, National Trust, Malvern Hills Conservators, Countryside Agency, Advantage West Midlands and Worcestershire and Herefordshire branches of CPRE.

English Heritage and the other organisations involved in this project also wish to express their gratitude to all the landowners who generously allowed access to their property.

English Heritage would also like to thank Mrs Carol Dolan for her generous contribution towards the costs of producing this book.

Summary

The Malvern Hills are a dramatic ridge of ancient volcanic rocks along the western edge of the Severn Valley, forming the boundary between the counties of Herefordshire and Worcestershire, and intruding into the northernmost parishes of Gloucestershire. Archaeologically, the Malvern Hills are known almost exclusively for the two very large and prominent Iron Age hillforts – British Camp and Midsummer Hill – that crown the ridge. In 1999 the Royal Commission on the Historical Monuments of England (now part of English Heritage) with a number of partners embarked on an investigative project in the area. This was designed to study the hillforts and other well-known sites around the Hills, but also to focus attention on the Hills as a landscape of special archaeological interest beyond these discrete 'sites'.

Comparatively little systematic archaeological research has been undertaken in the area previously – certainly in recent years – and this project fitted well the RCHME's (and EH's) desire to work closely with the managers of England's finest countryside. The project involved documentary research, aerial survey and fieldwork. The most significant results of the project are presented here and they will continue to inform management and conservation initiatives on and around the Hills through a Management Action and Monitoring Programme. They will also inform future research.

The Malverns have formed a boundary at least since the Bronze Age and it is this liminal, frontier aspect of the Hills that is emphasised here. This is not just a social or political phenomenon. It is stressed that, both in prehistory and in the medieval period, the Malverns were in effect a ritual landscape against which various religious rites were played out. The paramount importance of the numerous springs of pure water that issue from the Hills is crucial to this appreciation. The Malverns are not especially rich in the types of monuments that have traditionally drawn archaeologists, but by considering the landscape as a whole it is possible to draw legitimate inferences about the way in which the Hills might have been viewed and used by dwellers in the surrounding country.

Résumé

Les collines de Malvern sont une impressionnante crête de roches volcaniques anciennes le long de la rive ouest de la vallée de la Severn, et forment la frontière entre les comtés de Herefordshire et de Worcestershire, elles empiètent aussi sur les paroisses les plus au nord du comté de Gloucestershire. Sur le plan archéologique, la renommée des collines de Malvern repose presque exclusivement sur deux forteresses de sommet de colline datant de l'âge du fer – British Camp et Midsummer Hill – très étendues et occupant une place proéminente, elles couronnent la crête. En 1999, la Royal Commission on the Historical Monuments of England (Commission Royale pour les Monuments Historiques d'Angleterre) (qui fait maintenant partie d'English Heritage) s'embarqua avec un certain nombre de partenaires dans un programme de recherches dans la région. Il avait pour but d'étudier les forteresses et d'autres sites célèbres dans les alentours des collines, mais également de concentrer l'attention, au-delà de ces sites individuels, sur les collines en tant que paysage d'intérêt archéologique particulier. Comparativement peu de recherches archéologiques systématiques ont été entreprises dans la région auparavant – certainement au cours des années récentes – et ce projet s'harmonisait parfaitement avec le désir de RCHME (et d'EH) de travailler en étroite collaboration avec les gérants de la plus belle campagne d'Angleterre. Le projet comprenait des recherches documentaires, une prospection aérienne et un arpentage de terrain. Nous présentons ici les résultats les plus significatifs de ce projet et ils continueront à éclairer les initiatives de gestion et de conservation sur et aux alentours des collines grâce à un programme d'action et d'évaluation de cette gestion. Ils éclaireront également les recherches à venir. Les Malverns ont constitué une limite au moins depuis l'âge du bronze et c'est cet aspect de seuil, de frontière sur lequel nous insistons ici. Ce n'est pas seulement un phénomène social ou politique. Nous soulignons le fait qu'aussi bien à la préhistoire qu'à l'époque médiévale, les Malverns représentaient en réalité un paysage rituel sur le fond duquel se jouaient divers rites religieux. La suprême importance des sources d'eau pure qui sortent des collines est cruciale dans leur appréciation. Les Malverns ne sont pas particulièrement riches en ces types de monuments qui ont traditionnellement attiré les archéologues, mais si on considère le paysage dans son ensemble, il est possible de tirer des inférences légitimes sur la manière dont ces collines ont pu être perçues et utilisées par les habitants de la campagne environnante.

Traduction: Annie Pritchard

Zusammenfassung

Die Malvern Hills (Malverner Hügel) sind eine Hügelkette aus uraltem vulkanischen Gestein an der Westseite des Severn Valley. Sie bilden die Grenze zwischen den Grafschaften Herefordshire und Worcestershire und dringen in die nördlichsten Gemeinden von Gloucestershire ein. Aus archaeologischer Sicht sind die Malvern Hills fast exklusiv nur für die zwei aus dem Eisenzeitalter stammenden Hügelfestungen – British Camp und Midsummer Hill – bekannt, welche die Hügelkette krönen. Im Jahre 1999 begann die RCHME - Royal Commission on the Historical Monuments of England (Königliche Kommission für die historischen Monumente von England), mittlerweile zur Organisation EH - English Heritage (Englisches Erbtum) - gehörend, zusammen mit anderen Partnern ein Ermittlungsprojekt in diesem Gebiet. Dieses Unternehmen war darauf ausgerichtet, die Hügelfestungen und andere bereits bekannte Stätten zu studieren, aber auch um die Aufmersamkeit auf die Malvern Hills als eine Landschaft von speziellem archaeologischem Interesse über die bereits genannten Standorte hinaus zu lenken.

Vergleichsweise wenige systematische archaeologische Forschungen wurden in diesem Gebiet bereits ausgeführt – zumindestens in den letzten Jahren – und dieses Projekt paßte gut in das Verlangen von RCHME und EH mit den Managern von Englands feinsten Landschaften eng zusammen zu arbeiten. Das Projekt beinhaltete Literaturforschungen, Luftaufklärungen und Feldarbeiten. Die bedeutensten Resultate dieses Projektes werden hier präsentiert und sie werden in der Zukunft dazu dienen, Management- und Konservierungsinitiativen durch ein Managementaktions- und Überwachungs-programm zu informieren. Gleichzeitig dienen sie der Information für zukünftige Forschungen.

Die Malverns haben seit dem Bronzezeitalter eine Grenze gebildet und es ist dieser Grenzaspekt der Hügel, welcher hier verdeutlicht wird. Dieses ist nicht nur als soziales oder politisches Phänomen anzusehen. Es wird betont, daß in prähistorischen sowie in mittelalterlichen Zeiten die Malvern Hills im Effekt eine rituelle Landschaft war, gegen deren Hintergrund religiöse Riten ausgeführt wurden. Von höchster Wichtigkeit für das Verständnis dieser Tatsache sind die vielzähligen puren Naturwasserquellen, welche aus den Hügeln fliessen. Die Malverns sind nicht nur sehr reich an den Monumenten, welche traditionell Archaeologen anziehen, sondern auch durch die Betrachtung der Landschaft als Gesamtes ist es möglich, legitime Schlußfolgerungen über den Weg zu ziehen, in welchem die Hügel von Ansiedlern des benachbarten Umfelds betrachtet oder benutzt wurden.

Übersetzung: Norman Behrend

1
Introduction

The Hills

The Malvern Hills constitute one of the most distinctive topographical features in the whole of England. Viewed from the east they are visible from afar and are unmistakable, rising above the Severn Valley 'in Pyrramiddy fashion', to use Celia Fiennes' expressive phrase (Fig 1.1). Seen from the Herefordshire side they come as more of a surprise, being partly hidden by the broken nature of the terrain until close-to, but they are no less impressive for that.

The Hills have become a constituent part of the collective self-image of England through the cultural inspiration that they have provided in both literature and music. William Langland was a Malvernian and much has been made of the argument as to precisely where his 'Vision of Piers Plowman' occurred. More recently the name of Sir Edward Elgar has become inextricably linked to the Malvern landscape, which he loved and which inspired so much of his music.

Geology – origins of the land by David Field

The Malvern Hills form one of the most dramatic landforms in southern England and, compared to the scenery of the rest of the Severn drainage basin, and represent the culmination of intense tectonic movements and erosion. The faults, folds and thrusts indicate a multiplicity of episodes of enormous pressure, whose rocks attracted the attention of geologists long before serious study of the archaeology of the Hills took place. The field visits and papers of the Woolhope Club were dominated by geology from the time of its formation in 1851 and throughout the 1850s and 1860s, and were used as vehicles to explore the structure of the area. The banks of Midsummer hillfort were merely a vantage point to WS Symonds, who on one trip described the geology using his reversed hammer as a pointer (*Trans Woolhope Natur Field Club* [8] 1887, 1–3). Given the intensity of investigation, the unexplained trenching on the northern summit of Hollybush Hill (*see* Fig 2.13) might be the result of geological exploration. While studies of wider scope, including archaeology, were common from about 1877, the investigation of geology took pride of place through to the turn of the century (eg Calloway 1900; Conder 1898).

The great variety of rock forms has provided unrivalled opportunity for human exploitation of the area, though the topography itself has provided restrictions on activity within the landscape. The chain of hills provided a backdrop to the drift deposits of the Severn Valley river terraces, but also separated them from the undulating claylands to the west (Fig 1.2), providing two separate ecological and settlement zones. Clay from the Old Red Sandstone around Ledbury was thought to be used in a Beaker pot found on Midsummer Hill (Stanford 1981, 151) and dated to 2500–1700 BC, while another had incorporated Triassic materials found to the east of the hills. Medieval churches on both sides of the hills were constructed using local sandstone (eg RCHME 1932, 52, 61, 100, 141). Brick appears to have been used in local houses from at least the 17th century and, while the brickearths of the River Severn might conveniently have been used to the east of the hills, to the west there are restricted opportunities apart from the alluvium alongside the River Leadon. At the northern end of the Chain, the wide terrace of the River Teme bisects the hills and may have provided material for the potteries (*see* Chapter 2), while the river itself provided a means of shipping the finished goods. Both settlement pattern itself and the visible face of it are therefore, to some degree, a product of the resources available within the immediate environment.

Fig 1.1
The Malvern Hills are a long, narrow chain of peaks running south–north along the western edge of the Severn Valley. Clearly visible in this aerial view from the south are Chase End Hill, Ragged Stone Hill, Midsummer Hill, Herefordshire Beacon and, prominent in the distance, Worcestershire Beacon. The house in the foreground is Bromsberrow Place, a farmhouse remodelled and enlarged in the late 18th century and again in about 1825 – symbolic of increasing prosperity in the area.

In terms of early settlement, the area of the former lake basin around Colwall and the later Cradley Brook provided a focal point coupled with variety of soils. To the east, while some of the river terraces along the Severn would support agriculture, the areas of mudstone and solifluction debris were not well drained. The Severn at this point was tidal and consequently impeded drainage from the gravel fans around the base of the Malvern Hills. This resulted in waterlogging and the creation of large areas of marshland (Bond 1981, 95) now mapped as alluvium (BGS 1988).

Topography

The result of this geological history is a narrow, sierra-like, north–south range of hills rising to a height of 425m at the Worcestershire Beacon (Fig 1.3). The physical structure of the Hills also contributes one of its most significant and enduring features – the very purest spring water, which gushes from numerous fissures in the rock. This is not mineral water, but rain water. Weaver and Osborne (1994) list sixty or more springs, spouts, fountains and wells on the Malverns, but this is certainly an underestimate. The ridge forms a distinct boundary between the rolling Herefordshire landscape to the west (see Fig 1.2) and the low-lying, flat plain of Severn stretching away to Bredon Hill and the Cotswold escarpment to the east (Fig 1.4). The hills are a barrier, but one that is punctuated by a number of passes, notably at The Gullet, Wynds Point and The Wyche. Furthermore, the ridge is only 12km (8.5 miles) long. The hills do not therefore block Herefordshire from Worcestershire practically, but they do mark a symbolic boundary. The radically different topography on either side is reflected in very different agricultural and social histories.

The generally well-wooded ridges of the Suckley Hills, Storridge Common, Wellington Heath, Frith Wood and so on dominate the western side. To the east, with the exception of a few low hills (particularly to the south between Eldersfield and Castlemorton), the topography is relatively flat and dominated by the lowland commons such as Hollybed and Castlemorton (Fig 1.5). These commons are rare survivals in lowland England. Beyond these was Longdon Marsh and, although it lay almost entirely outside the current study area, its

significance cannot be ignored. The group of basins in the Mercia Mudstone (formerly Keuper Marl), in which the marsh developed, are fed by the springs on the eastern flank of the Malverns but, before the mid-19th century, were also periodically inundated by estuarine water when the Severn was in flood. The result was a brackish marsh, notable for its salt-tolerant flora, though well inland (Bond 1981). The difference between the eastern and western flanks of the hills extends to urban topography – medieval Ledbury contrasts strongly with early-Victorian Malvern.

History

The history of the Malvern Hills is dominated by its two hillforts, its two towns and its two priories. Although the hillforts are dominant features in the landscape and have exercised the imagination of Malvernians through the centuries, history has nothing to tell of their true story. They belong to prehistory, and archaeology alone is the key to understanding them. The towns, Ledbury and Malvern, as hinted above, have very different stories (Hillaby 1997; B Smith 1978).

Ledbury grew up in the shadow of its minster church and at the crossing of two major routes in the early medieval period. A new borough was created by the Bishop of Hereford at this rural market centre in the early 12th century. The town still retains recognisably the plan that it was given at this time. Meanwhile, at Malvern there were only small rural settlements at 'Baldenhall' (Hall Green) and Malvern Link. The Benedictine priory at Great Malvern was founded on remote wasteland, more than a mile from 'Baldenhall', in the 1080s, a daughter house of Westminster. Although the priory flourished it did not attract urban development. By 1800, when Malvern was already known as a spa, it was still only a village and it was not until the middle of the 19th century that it developed into a town. The priory at Little Malvern, also a Benedictine foundation, began in about 1125 and was at first closely connected to Great Malvern, but was soon a cell of Worcester. It, too, was and remained in a location apparently remote from other settlement. Both priories occupied similar positions, towards the foot of the steeper slopes and below significant springs.

The hills were surrounded by numerous smaller agricultural settlements on the lower ground, most of which remain in the landscape today. However, much of the area in the medieval period was taken up by chases and deerparks. It was a well-wooded landscape, as evidenced by the numerous 'field', 'leah' and 'haga' place names suggesting clearings and woodland enclosures. The hilltops – the 'moel bryn' or 'bald hill' – on the other hand were already, and probably had been for a long time (Gelling 1978, 52), grazing land, perhaps held in common. More commons existed over the 'moors' and marsh to the east of the hills. A 'medieval' rural scene survived late around the Malverns and it is not until well on into the conventional 'post-medieval' period that disafforestation (the reduction of the legal status of land from forest to ordinary land), the draining of the marshes and the creation of a 'landscape of leisure' around the spa brought major changes.

Water is a recurrent feature in the history of the Malvern Hills. The quackery of the 'Water Cure' led to the rapid growth of Great Malvern in the later 19th century, but the numerous holy wells around the hills were already important places in the medieval period, running water is central to Piers Plowman's dreaming, and water was certainly a significant factor in the layout of the hillfort at Midsummer Hill in the Iron Age.

The Hills have also attracted many myths and legends. Some of these are just amusing fairy stories, such as that concerning the rock-throwing giant, Clutter. Others are pleasant, though false, versions of history, such as the story that British Camp was the scene of Caractacus' last stand against the Romans, which originated with a prominent 19th-century vicar of Great Malvern, the Reverend Henry Card (B Smith 1978, 9–10). This myth at least had the happy effect of informing Elgar's *Caractacus*, which was written at Birchwood, Storridge and inspired by the view of British Camp from the composer's mother's cottage at Colwall. Other myths are persistent misapprehensions. Into this category falls the rather ingenious derivation of the name 'Colwall' from the Latin 'collis', a hill, and 'vallum', a wall, with the idea that this refers to British Camp. The name, first recorded as 'Colewelle', probably means 'cool well, stream or spring' (Ekwall 1960, 118; B Smith 1978, 13), which while at first glance appearing more mundane, nevertheless has potentially interesting historical and literary associations.

Fig 1.6
H H Lines was one of a small group of local antiquarians who first studied the monuments on the Hills in the later 19th century; this is one of his sketches of British Camp, dated 1860 (Society of Antiquaries of London).

Previous archaeological research and the current project

Although many ancient sites are well known (Fig 1.6) and a number of discoveries have been made on and around the Malverns, the district has not been subject to very much systematic antiquarian and archaeological work in the past. In recent years the excavations by Dr S C Stanford at Midsummer Hill (1981) and fieldwork by the RCHME (1932), by Bond (1978; 1981) and by Dyer (1990) stand out as exceptions. Before that it is necessary to go back to the work of Hilton Price at British Camp in the

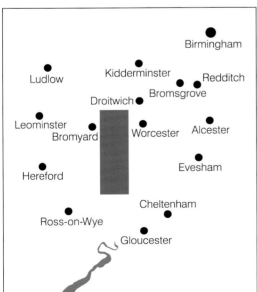

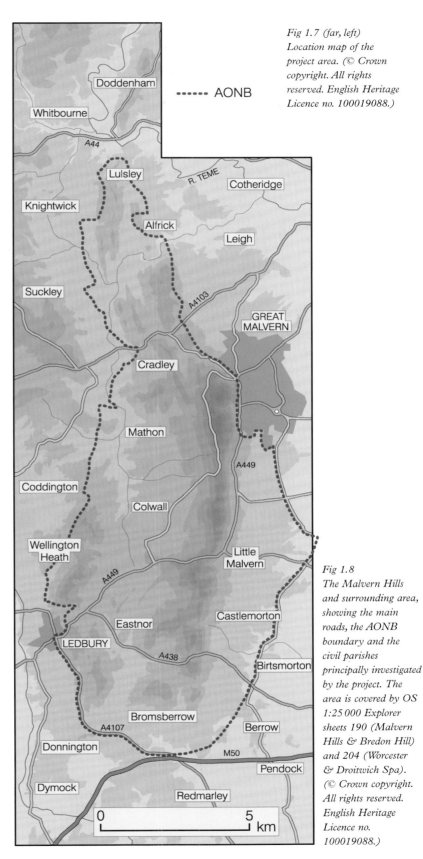

Fig 1.7 (far, left) Location map of the project area. (© Crown copyright. All rights reserved. English Heritage Licence no. 100019088.)

Fig 1.8 The Malvern Hills and surrounding area, showing the main roads, the AONB boundary and the civil parishes principally investigated by the project. The area is covered by OS 1:25 000 Explorer sheets 190 (Malvern Hills & Bredon Hill) and 204 (Worcester & Droitwich Spa). (© Crown copyright. All rights reserved. English Heritage Licence no. 100019088.)

Fig 1.9
The sign erected at British Camp by the Malvern Hills Conservators. Although the information is not entirely erroneous, it serves as a warning not to set archaeological theories in stone. The sign is now itself a historical monument of some interest.

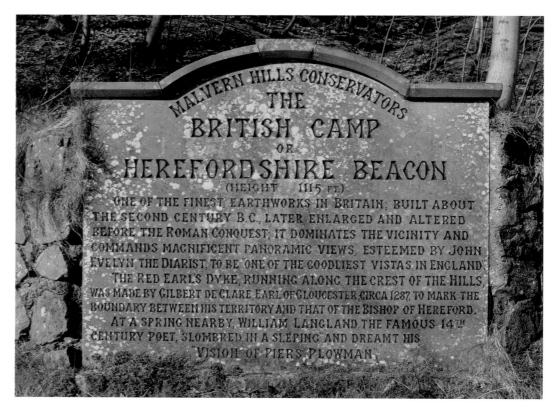

MALVERN HILLS CONSERVATORS
THE
BRITISH CAMP
OR
HEREFORDSHIRE BEACON
(HEIGHT 1115 FT)
ONE OF THE FINEST EARTHWORKS IN BRITAIN; BUILT ABOUT THE SECOND CENTURY B.C., LATER ENLARGED AND ALTERED BEFORE THE ROMAN CONQUEST; IT DOMINATES THE VICINITY AND COMMANDS MAGNIFICENT PANORAMIC VIEWS, ESTEEMED BY JOHN EVELYN THE DIARIST, TO BE ONE OF THE GOODLIEST VISTAS IN ENGLAND. THE RED EARL'S DYKE, RUNNING ALONG THE CREST OF THE HILLS, WAS MADE BY GILBERT DE CLARE EARL OF GLOUCESTER CIRCA 1287, TO MARK THE BOUNDARY BETWEEN HIS TERRITORY AND THAT OF THE BISHOP OF HEREFORD. AT A SPRING NEARBY, WILLIAM LANGLAND, THE FAMOUS 14TH CENTURY POET, SLOMBRED IN A SLEPING AND DREAMT HIS VISION OF PIERS PLOWMAN.

1870s (1887) to find anything similar. Otherwise archaeological knowledge of the area, prior to the project reported here, comes largely from chance finds and casual observations.

In 1999 the Royal Commission on the Historical Monuments of England (now part of English Heritage) initiated a project to study the archaeological monuments and landscapes of the Malvern Hills and surrounding area (Figs 1.7 and 1.8). This project was intended to promote a new view of the archaeology of the Malverns, one that is about the fabric of the landscape as created and modified over a long time period and in which our own choices and activities are part of that continuum. This contrasts with a more traditional view of archaeology that is populated only by discrete sites and established categories of artefacts. It is more important to change perceptions and frames of thought than simply to add 'new' sites to the record, although of course that is also part of the activity. This aspiration reflects the changing nature of archaeology as a discipline that is increasingly concerned with its relationship to land-use management and to public understanding. The project was undertaken as a joint exercise by staff of English Heritage and colleagues from the relevant county archaeological services. Some details of the methods employed are given in Appendix 2.

This book aims to present the significant results of the project and to celebrate the special landscape of the Malverns but it is not, and could never be, a definitive statement. Archaeological research will continue, new discoveries will be made, new questions and ideas formulated. Archaeology as a discipline does not deal in unique and fixed historical truths (Fig 1.9). Perceptions legitimately change, which is why the creation of records is an intrinsic part of archaeological activity, enabling re-interpretation of the evidence in the future. Understanding of past human endeavour on the Malvern Hills will continue to develop and change.

2
Prehistoric and Romano-British periods

Early prehistory (to 4000 BC)

The Palaeolithic period, or Old Stone Age (down to 10,000 BC), is characterised in Britain by the activities, between Ice Ages, of groups of hunter-gatherers. In the succeeding Mesolithic (Middle Stone Age: 10,000–4000 BC), after the last Ice Age, deciduous woodlands developed on what had been tundra landscapes. Sea levels rose and Britain became an island by 8000 BC. People continued to live by hunting and gathering in this changing environment. Finds of these remote periods are rare generally, and the Malvern region is no exception. The earliest evidence for human activity in this area is provided by a single Palaeolithic handaxe and four findspots of Mesolithic material (Fig 2.1).

The handaxe is an ovate form of Middle Acheulian date (c 300,000–200,000 BC), found just to the north of Colwall Stone in a ploughed field (Wymer 1996, 193) on a gravel surface overlooking the basin of a former lake. The axe was in fresh condition, suggesting that it has not moved far from its original place of deposition. Other finds of Palaeolithic date have been found just outside the project area at Hanley Castle and Worcester.

Two blades or flakes of Mesolithic date have been found, also in ploughed land, to the north of the Eastnor obelisk (SO 73 NE 22). Another blade or flake was found at Meadow Farm, Stanford Bishop, (Wymer with Bonsall 1977, 126) but the findspot is not certain and it may lie just outside the project area. A large quantity of flint flakes found between Worcestershire Beacon and North Hill are said to have included some of Mesolithic character but they have been lost (SO 75 NE 127) and nothing further can be said about them. Other Mesolithic finds, including twenty-three blades or flakes and a scraper, are said to have been found near Welsh House Farm, Dymock (Wymer with Bonsall 1977, 101).

This sparse record of activity for the earliest prehistoric periods appears disappointing, but the significance of the handaxe lies in its condition, suggesting that there may be further evidence of Palaeolithic activity awaiting discovery at this location. The fact that this handaxe and much of the Mesolithic material were found in arable land also suggests that a programme of systematic fieldwalking would yield further results (*see* Chapter 4).

The Neolithic and Bronze Age (4000–700 BC)

Neolithic and Earlier Bronze Age

The Neolithic, or New Stone Age, and Earlier Bronze Age (4000–1500 BC), is the period during which agriculture was first introduced to Britain, bringing with it the first move towards sedentary communities. Those communities, increasingly associated with particular places, began to build monumental structures associated with the ancestors and with celestial bodies – causewayed enclosures and long barrows, henges and stone circles. It is also the period in which pottery was first used in Britain and in which the development of stone technology became increasingly refined, culminating in ground and polished stone axes.

Metal – copper and bronze – was first used for tools, weapons and ornaments from about 2500 BC. Bronze did not completely replace flint and other stone for tool making, however. The waning of the Neolithic period also saw changes in social structure marked by the replacement of communal burial by the burial of pre-eminent individuals, often beneath round mounds. This change was accompanied by an array of new artefacts – initially beaker pots, barbed-and-tanged arrowheads and fine ornaments. Later the beakers were replaced by a series of urn types. Settlement sites of the Earlier Bronze Age, as in the Neolithic, are hard to identify.

Neolithic

The Neolithic is represented in the study area by a wide scatter of chance finds (Fig 2.2). No structures certainly of this date are known, although any of the ring ditches conventionally

Fig 2.1
Distribution map of
Palaeolithic and
Mesolithic finds. (Based
on an Ordnance Survey
map. © Crown copyright.
All rights reserved.
English Heritage licence
no. 100019088.)

Fig 2.2
Distribution map of
Neolithic finds. (Based on
an Ordnance Survey
map. © Crown copyright.
All rights reserved.
English Heritage licence
no. 100019088.)

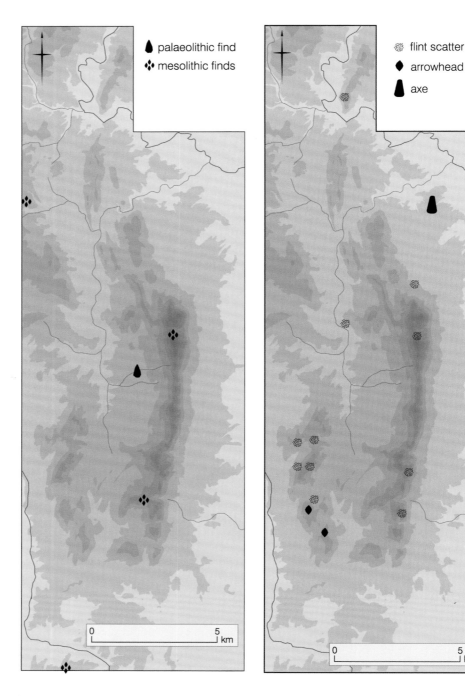

dated to the Bronze Age *could* be of Neolithic origin (Fig 2.3). The Malverns fall within a wide gap in the distribution of causewayed enclosures, and the megalithic tombs that are so prevalent on the Cotswolds were not built here. Later Neolithic monuments, such as henges and stone circles, are also unknown in this part of England.

Large scatters of debris from flint tool making have been found between Frith Wood, Ledbury, and Wellington Heath; at Hope End, Colwall; on Hangman's Hill; on Midsummer Hill; between the Worcestershire Beacon and North Hill; at West Malvern and Cowleigh Park; and on Ankerdine Hill, Doddenham. Single finds and small groups are scattered widely across the area. The flint was, of course, imported from outside the area; the nearest source is the Marlborough Downs. Among these waste flakes and cores are a few finished tools – nearly all scrapers (small tools probably used in the preparation of hides), although there is a re-used fragment of a ground axe at Midsummer

Hill (Bowen 1949, 35; Brown 1961, 83–4; H Moore 1896).

Two arrowheads have also been found, both at Eastnor (Robinson 1971). One is of the type known as a 'petit tranchet derivative', developed from a Mesolithic form but, in this instance, probably of later Neolithic date. The other is a lozenge-shaped arrowhead, which has been

worked to produce a slight tang for fixing it to a shaft – again this is probably of a late Neolithic date. A ground stone axe, probably originating in South Wales, was found at Sherridge, Leigh (*Trans Worcs Archaeol Soc* **35**, 1958, 77).

These finds are enough to show that the landscape was widely (if not intensively) used in the Neolithic period, but not enough to suggest any detail about the activities that were carried out. The arrowheads might imply hunting and the scrapers, perhaps, hide preparation. The single axe might – but need not – be evidence for woodland clearance. The apparent absence of any monumental remains of this period is striking (although it has to be remembered that major monuments are rare in many regions, and that Neolithic activity is more typically represented by scattered finds and small features). It seems unlikely now that the absence of major Neolithic sites in this region can be put down simply to lack of research. It begins to look as

Fig 2.3
Double ring ditch with associated pits, near Aubrey's Farm, Bromsberrow. (Based on an Ordnance Survey map. © Crown copyright. All rights reserved. English Heritage licence no. 100019088.)

Fig 2.4
Unlike British Camp (in the foreground) and the relatively slight Pinnacle Hill (middle distance) the higher northern Hills were never built on in prehistoric times (with the possible exception of the Shire Ditch) – possibly they were regarded as being too sacred to be disturbed.

though the Malverns, and indeed much of Herefordshire and Worcestershire, were little used at this time, and usage differed from some neighbouring regions – notably Gloucestershire and Warwickshire. In the case of the Malverns this may reflect the difficulty of this area – high dramatic hills with fast-flowing springs and marshes at their foot – for primary agricultural exploitation and its attraction, conversely, as an interface with a world of spirits.

The lack of monuments of this date on the Malvern ridge requires explanation – were the hills too sacred even for the construction of sacred monuments (Bradley 2000)? If so it is remarkable that some of them, especially Worcestershire Beacon and the northern group of hills, apparently remained free of monuments throughout prehistory – these are the highest peaks in the range (Fig 2.4). Though there have been suggestions that there were burial mounds on North Hill and Table Hill (B Smith1978, 5) these cannot be substantiated. The lack of monuments perhaps reflects the position of the Malvern ridge as part of a developing boundary zone along the Severn and its tributaries. However, it might be that natural features – prominent hilltops, springs, bogs – were the focus for ceremonies and activities that did not generate field monuments of a type traditionally recognised by archaeologists.

Earlier Bronze Age

The 'Beaker' period is represented by a handful of beaker sherds associated with some small hollows excavated on Hollybush Hill, which the excavator considered to represent domestic activity (Stanford 1981, 137–8). Two barbed-and-tanged flint arrowheads of the same period were found in the garden of the Police Station at West Malvern in 1937. They were described as being in perfect condition (SO 74 NE 32) and were therefore probably from a burial, the rest of which is presumably yet to be found. Another find of the transitional period from Neolithic to Bronze Age date is a square-butted flint axe, possibly of Scandinavian origin, found on the hills above Colwall (Piggott 1938, 101). Worked flints, including arrowheads and a scraper possibly of Bronze Age date, have been found between North Hill and End Hill (Bowen 1949, 35).

In the 1930s discoveries were made in a sandpit at Mathon, where Later Bronze Age cremations had been found earlier (see below). Finds included a stone battle axe head and urns (Hamilton 1940), one of them a collared urn, which could date anywhere between 2200 BC and 1400 BC. One of the urns contained some fragments of cremated human bone. There was

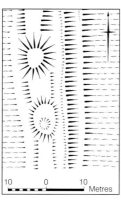

no sign of a barrow here, but aerial photography has revealed ring ditches, almost certainly the remains of round barrows, at Ledbury, Redmarley d'Abitot, Dymock and Donnington (Fig 2.5). These are in addition to the two mounds on the Malvern ridge at Pinnacle Hill, which have been recorded as barrows or cairns (Fig 2.6). These are probably all Bronze Age funerary monuments but again caution must be exercised – any of the ring ditches could prove to be of earlier, Neolithic, date. The most significant is possibly the double ring ditch with

flints
barrows/ring ditches
enclosures
cemetery
metal finds
hut circles
field systems
Shire Ditch

associated pits at Aubrey's Farm, Bromsberrow (*see* Fig 2.3). Whether or not this is late Neolithic in origin the double ring and pits suggest a certain longevity of use within the Bronze Age.

The two mounds on Pinnacle Hill pose a different problem. They have clearly been regarded as ancient burial mounds in the past, as the southernmost one in particular shows signs of having been dug into. No excavations are recorded, however. The mounds may be of some antiquity, but their relationship to the Shire Ditch is unclear; it is not possible to tell from surface indications alone whether they are cut by the ditch or whether they overlie its bank. If they are barrows or cairns, they stand out as being possibly unique on the Malvern ridge. It may be relevant that Pinnacle Hill is one of the more insignificant of the Malvern peaks. When a cremation under a cup and other adult human remains were buried on the summit of the Worcestershire Beacon towards the middle of the Bronze Age (Allies 1852, 67; Blake 1913, 92), it is doubtful whether a mound was raised over them – possibly the height and regular conical shape of the hill itself was thought to render any such construction superfluous.

It is important to note the exact circumstances of the recovery of these cremations. They were found by a soldier of the Royal Ordnance Corps in 1849, while he was digging in a cairn on the summit of the hill. The reason for his activities, that he and his comrades were looking for the datum

point previously placed there during the Trigonometrical Survey, seems to indicate that the cairn was of recent origin. However, the accounts are slightly ambiguous on this point, and interpretation depends on whether the datum mark had been made on bedrock or on a stone within a pre-existing cairn. The cremation on the southern side of the cairn was partly under a small inverted 'pygmy cup' (Fig 2.7), while that on the northern side was not associated with any artefact.

Bradlow Knoll at the southern end of Frith Wood, Ledbury, presents another intriguing possibility for the location of a Bronze Age burial mound. The place name itself is suggestive, 'low' often deriving from Old English 'hlaw', a burial mound. There is, in fact, a circular mound, which appears to be artificial, on Bradlow Knoll (Hoverd 2003, 28).

Later Bronze Age

In the Later Bronze Age (1500–700 BC) burials became less elaborate and there was an increased emphasis, in many areas, on enclosed settlement and the development of a more clearly demarcated agricultural landscape of fields and, after about 1000 BC, linear earthwork boundaries.

There are some indications of the presence of an earthwork enclosure pre-dating the hillfort on Midsummer Hill (*see* Fig 2.13). To the west of the northern entrance a ledge curves inside the Iron Age rampart and appears to underlie it. Around much of the circuit on Hollybush Hill are remnants of a similar ledge. To the south the scarp of this ledge becomes stronger and curves uphill around the southern end of the hillfort, but is now obscured by a later track. Where the Shire Ditch approaches the hillfort in the north, one element lies over both this ledge and the counterscarp of the hillfort. The antiquarian H H Lines seems to have observed this feature in 1869, notably at the north-eastern corner of Hollybush Hill. In his plan (Lines nd) it clearly runs under the counterscarp bank at the southern end of Hollybush. This feature could represent a substantial Later Bronze Age hilltop enclosure. Though no artefacts of this period have been recovered in excavations, this remains at least a possibility.

There are several other enclosures revealed by aerial photography (*see* Fig 2.15), and some of these might be settlements of Later Bronze Age date, although they are perhaps more likely to belong to the Iron Age. Additionally, there are two places where small circular features,

Fig 2.7
Drawing of the miniature urn found on the Worcestershire Beacon with cremated human remains in 1849; scale 1:4 (originally published in the Archaeol J *7, 1850, opposite p66).*

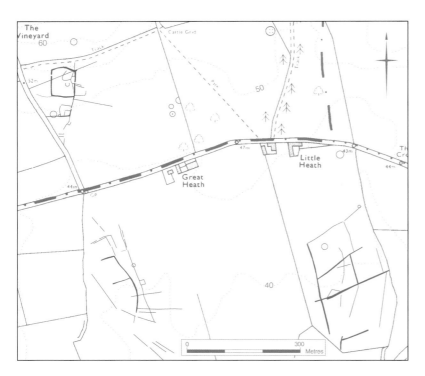

and ashes were contained in fragmentary urns, of a type dating to 1500–1000 BC, these were placed at the eastern end of the areas of burning. In some cases small upright stone slabs surrounded the whole burnt area. Some unburnt human bones and a tooth were also found. The tips of two bronze spearheads were recovered from among masses of burnt material. Other finds included worked flints and part of a possible quernstone.

This site occupies a low but locally significant eminence above the Cradley Brook but is almost surrounded by higher hills. Another urn found some 500m to the south-west, also on a local rise, was close to a small circular enclosure subsequently revealed by aerial photography. This had been an area of some significance at least since the beginning of the Bronze Age, as indicated by the deposit of a battle axe and a cremation in a collared urn (mentioned above).

Other chance finds of this period from the hills include a fragment of a bronze sword and part of a bronze razor, both found, apparently, in a quarry to the north of the Wyche Cutting. Two bronze palstaves (axe heads) have also been found, one on Malvern Link Common and the other at West Malvern. Unfortunately, both are now lost, but the one from West Malvern was illustrated by Blake (1914). This probably dates to about 1400–1200 BC and the other is very probably of similar date.

Perhaps the most intriguing possibility concerning the Bronze Age discovered by the project relates to the Shire Ditch (Fig 2.9). Although the medieval date for the creation of this prominent earthwork suggested by the documentary evidence has generally been accepted, this has by no means been universal. As long ago as the 1870s Hilton Price suggested that it might be of prehistoric origin (1887, 226–7). Fieldwork at Midsummer Hill during the current project has produced support for that view through the observation that where the Shire Ditch meets the hillfort ramparts it is of two phases (*see* Fig 2.13). A prominent but narrow ditch, with a corresponding bank to the east, is mirrored by a bank and ditch of shallow profile immediately adjacent to the west. The difference in profile of the two ditches appears to indicate that the western is older than the eastern. This is confirmed at the junction with the hillfort earthworks, where the shallow western ditch apparently underlies the earliest hillfort scarp.

In contrast, the eastern ditch cuts across both the ledge of the postulated Later Bronze Age hilltop enclosure and the Iron Age hillfort counterscarp. The first phase of the Shire Ditch

too small to be barrows, have been recorded by aerial photography. These possible unenclosed round houses are both at Donnington. They are 7m to 9m in diameter and in both cases appear to be overlain by elements of field systems (Fig 2.8) that could also be of later prehistoric date, possibly between 1500 BC and 1000 BC (although they could also be of considerably later date). These rectangular fields are bounded by ditches and measure approximately 115m by 90m.

A group of small platforms on a steep west-facing slope was discovered in Frith Wood adjacent to an area of very small lynchets, where disturbed soil has built up against a boundary (Hoverd 2000a). These features could represent another small Bronze Age settlement with its fields. Unenclosed settlement in association with field systems is a typical feature of the Later Bronze Age in this part of England (T Moore forthcoming a). None of these features is securely dated, however, and they might belong to the succeeding Iron Age or Romano-British periods. Only excavation can resolve this question.

The most striking remains of a Bronze Age cemetery in the area were found at South End, Mathon. Here the digging of sandpits in the early years of the 20th century revealed human remains. About fifteen cremations were recorded and it was noted that about thirty more had already been destroyed (Blake 1913). The cremated remains were deposited in distinct burnt areas. In cases where the cremated bones

Fig 2.9
The Shire Ditch. Although
the earthwork here is
undated, the boundary
that it marks is probably
late Bronze Age in origin.

must therefore pre-date the hillfort. (At British Camp, it should be noted, the relationship between the Shire Ditch and the hillfort defences is unclear but the existing Ditch seems to overlie the counterscarp at the south-east side of the enlarged fort.)

A similar ridge-top boundary bank and ditch has been discovered in the course of the project in Frith Wood. This appears to respect the postulated barrow at Bradlow Knoll and could also be of Later Bronze Age date. It is certainly not later than the early medieval period (Hoverd 2000a; 2003, 28, 40). Similar features have been noted along the ridge tops of the Suckley Hills (Hoverd 2003, 37). Another boundary feature dating to the Later Bronze Age has been discovered to the west of the Chase High School, Malvern (Griffin *et al* 2000, 6 et passim). A small ditch, running perpendicular to the line of the hills (and therefore to the Shire Ditch), had been deliberately backfilled, perhaps by the levelling of an associated bank. This backfill contained pottery of both Later Bronze Age and Early Iron Age date, as well as cattle teeth and an elderberry seed. The Bronze Age pottery was fresh and unabraded. The excavators considered that the evidence indicated a Late Bronze Age date for the cutting of the ditch. It was backfilled in the Early Iron Age or later, but certainly before the Roman period. On analogy with the rest of the

Severn–Cotswold region (T Moore forthcoming a) and Wessex (McOmish *et al* 2002, 56–65) – where linear ditches are a feature of the Later Bronze Age landscape – it may be that the Malvern Hills and the adjacent ridges were also divided at this early period.

The increasing importance of land division, through the creation of field systems and boundaries, was an important feature of the period and this appears now to be reflected in the Malverns. Another significant theme of Later Bronze Age society in Britain is the conspicuous consumption of wealth through the deliberate deposition of bronze. Valuable metal objects were buried or cast away in locations from which they could not be recovered, perhaps as gifts to the gods, but certainly also as an act symbolising the wealth and power of the individual. This practice probably explains the deposition of the two palstaves and possibly the other bronze finds noted above. Control over access to such items and the restricted raw materials (and skills) required to make them, and the ability to discard them, were clearly sources of prestige. Though the exact findspots are not known, the significance of these objects is that they were deposited on the ridge or on relatively high ground, albeit in areas where the distinctiveness of the location is admittedly not now obvious.

The Iron Age (700 BC–AD 43)

Climatic change, economic crisis and social upheaval marked the last centuries of the Bronze Age in Britain. In the past such economic and social shifts were explained as being the result of invasions, but the activities of the indigenous population are now thought to be more likely drivers of change. The climatic deterioration is also, no doubt, a factor but its importance should not be exaggerated. A breakdown in the control of the bronze supply, perhaps in part fuelled by the competitive consumption mentioned above, caused a shift in power and prestige. The discovery that edged tools, weapons and ornaments could also be made from the much more readily available iron ores, no doubt speeded the collapse of the bronze exchange systems. At the same time the land divisions established during the period might have started to break down. The transition from what we recognise as Bronze Age to Iron Age was undoubtedly protracted, but some of the changes were profound, not least the construction of the very prominent new hillforts.

In and around the Malvern Hills the Iron Age, or perhaps the latest Bronze Age, gives us the first obvious, conspicuous monuments in the landscape (Fig 2.10). The Malverns are situated well within a zone dominated by hillforts, stretching from the chalk downs of southern England through the Marches to North Wales.

Hillforts

The two great hillforts of Midsummer Hill and British Camp dominate the archaeological landscape of the Malverns, but there are in fact five hillforts within the project area. Two sites have been struck off the list. As a result of previous investigation and work for this project it is clear that the earthworks at 'Kilbury Camp' near Ledbury are cultivation remains and not the remains of a hillfort. It has been suggested that there is a hillfort at Poplands Farm, Whitbourne (Sawle 1981; Williams 1979, 14, 16, 22), but no convincing evidence has been produced and it is possible that the earthworks there, such as they are, relate to a medieval deer park. On the other hand, the hillfort at Berrow Hill, Martley, previously regarded as 'doubtful', was confirmed as a genuine hillfort by project fieldwork. The remaining two sites are Haffield Camp, Donnington, and Gadbury Bank, Eldersfield. These are both small forts surrounded by single ramparts. Both are currently (and have been for some time) under dense tree cover and no recent

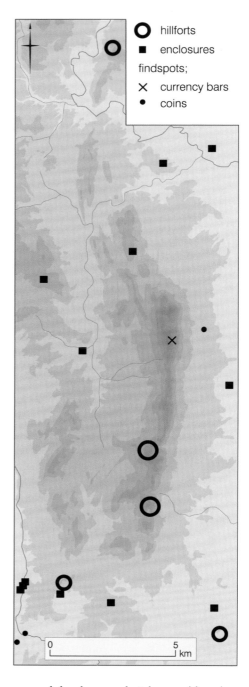

research has been undertaken at either site.

Of these sites only Midsummer Hill has been systematically excavated (Stanford 1981) and this is therefore the only one for which there is any dating evidence, although even here it is slight. Elsewhere in southern Britain hillforts are known to have been constructed during the Later Bronze Age but most were probably built from 600 BC onwards with some major changes around 400 BC and abandonment at or soon after 100 BC.

where it is discernible at all, is very slight. This might partly be due to hillwash from the interior masking it, but clearly it was never a high rampart. There is a suggestion at one or two places of internal quarrying to obtain material for the rampart, but nothing in the nature of the extensive quarry ditches seen at many other hillforts (including Midsummer Hill). Significantly, the rampart backscarp is most persistently present, and highest, in proximity to the entrances. At the western entrance it is up to 1m high.

The relationships between the two phases of hillfort are difficult to unpick in detail, although the broad outline is clear. On the west and north-west sides of the early fort the second phase rampart is identical with its predecessor, but the ditch has been deepened, leaving the first phase ditch 'hanging' where the earthworks of the two phases part company (c). The second phase rampart butts uncomfortably half way up the first phase escarpment at this point, with its backscarp sealing off the now-redundant first-phase ditch. On the eastern side, however, it is the counterscarp of the earlier fort that has been utilised as the second-phase rampart, with a new ditch dug below and the redundant first-phase rampart left above as a scarp. The continuous second-phase ramparts in this area connect the enclosure of the southern and north-eastern spurs and, crucially, show that both spurs were brought within the fort at the same time. The reason for the difference of treatment to east and west appears to be that the defences of the earlier fort were tilted to the contours, so that the top of the rampart on the west side was approximately level with the top of the counterscarp on the east.

There is an indication that the plans for the second phase defences on the eastern side of the hill were changed during construction. The counterscarp of the early fort can be seen to the west of (d), but this scarp then turns to the south, following the contours of the hill around a slight combe. It looks as though the rampart of the second phase was intended to follow the same line and there are indications that construction on this line had commenced. However, after work on scarping the slopes had begun, it was decided to run the defences straight across the combe, regardless of the contours. The abandoned scarping remains as evidence of this change of mind. This change of plan in the laying out of the second-phase defences on the eastern side could have been to include an area of sheltered, useable ground that, although it exhibits no recognisable hut circles, could have been occupied. Alternatively, the ramparts could have been re-aligned to

create an entrance, which would have been difficult to construct on the higher line.

There are four original entrances to the second phase hillfort. All have enlarged rampart terminals and slightly overlapping counterscarp terminals. The northern entrance (e) is no longer easy to see, as it has been disturbed by the recent construction of metalled paths and stone retaining walls. Its presence is only indicated by a mis-alignment of the counterscarp, but its existence is confirmed by a plan and description by the RCHME (1932, 55–6) before the paths were made. It is unusual for a hillfort to have four entrances and this may reflect the considerable length of this site. It is notable that while two of the entrances are at the extreme north and south ends of the site they have been contrived to face east, conforming to the general preference for east- or west-facing entrances, noted above.

As many as 118 probable or possible circular building platforms have been identified within the second-phase hillfort and many more might have existed in the relatively flat areas to the south of Millennium Hill where earthworks will not have formed readily. In a few examples these stances have elongated sub-rectangular platforms alongside them, of a type that has also been recognised at Midsummer Hill (see below). Whether these represent the sites of subsidiary structures, or yards or gardens, is uncertain. Not all the round buildings will have been intended for human occupation, nor can it be assumed that they were all in contemporary use, although, as at Midsummer Hill, there is scarce evidence for chronological depth – the majority of the buildings now visible could all relate to a single phase of use.

The huts are clustered into groups but no strong patterning emerges, although the long 'terrace' lines of huts in the northern part of the hillfort are unusual and striking. Numerous four-post structures have been excavated on other Herefordshire hillforts and the possibility that these were present at British Camp, alongside the circular buildings, should be borne in mind. Also of interest is a possible spring (f), which lies near the bottom of the first-phase ditch and which will have been brought within the hillfort by the later extension. It consists only of a hollow declivity in the bedrock and can never have been a useable water supply, but the soil below it was observed to be damp at the time of the survey, when the ground was otherwise dry.

None of these features is securely dated. The first-phase hillfort is probably of Early Iron Age date but might be of the Later Bronze Age or even earlier. The second-phase hillfort is most likely to be of the Middle Iron Age – a major increase in the size of hillforts is a common occurrence in the Marches and elsewhere at about 400 BC.

Midsummer Hill

Midsummer Hill is the best known of the Malvern hillforts, largely owing to Dr Stanford's excavations (1981). Despite this basis of sound existing knowledge, the present survey (Field 2000) has added much detail to the history of the site (Fig 2.13).

The site is exceptional in that the ramparts enclose two adjacent summits and an intervening valley. Midsummer Hill itself is the higher but a geological fault has displaced it, like Herefordshire Beacon, from the axis of the main ridge. The ravine-like valley provides the easiest approach and it is here that the main, south-facing, entrance to the fort (a) lies. This is also the position of a spring, which might have contributed much to shaping this part of the natural landscape. Today it is merely a trickle, but in the Iron Age it might have been much more imposing.

The enclosing earthworks comprise a single bank with external ditch and a small counterscarp bank. In between the two hills they are carried up severe gradients in order to complete the circuit. While the rampart is generally only about 1m high internally, it is so positioned on the break of the slope that it is up to 11m above the ditch. An internal quarry ditch, for rampart material, can be traced around much of the circuit, particularly on Hollybush Hill. Two entrances appear to be original. At the northern end of Midsummer Hill there is a rather narrow oblique entrance between inturned rampart terminals (b). At the southern end of the ravine both rampart terminals are inturned for at least 10m, forming a narrow corridor. Extensive excavations here revealed seventeen phases of construction, repair, re-design and renewal dating from 470 BC to AD 30, according to the excavator (Stanford 1981, 56–60). It should be noted, however, that this chronological scheme is based on only two radiocarbon dates, and a much shorter time span may be more realistic. Early plans (Lines nd; Hughes 1926, f18) indicate an entrance at the southern end of Hollybush but are contradictory as to whether it was original or not, and this evidence has been quarried away. Other breaks through the ramparts appear to be later in date.

No fewer than 483 platforms, mostly circular, were recorded in the interior of the hillfort. These are interpreted as building platforms contemporary with the hillfort. They occur on both hills, often arranged in rows along the contours. This is particularly clear on the eastern slopes of Midsummer Hill, where they are arranged on at least ten terraces that roughly follow the contours of the hillside. In part these terraces may reflect the underlying geology, but they have been considerably enhanced by human modifications and not only provide level positions for houses, but also for yards or gardens.

A few possible house stances are situated in the ravine outside the south gate of the hillfort, three of them overlying the counterscarp bank. The extent of these was not great, however, and the 'British Town' marked on antiquarian plans (eg Piper 1898) cannot be traced. It seems likely that the features interpreted by antiquarian investigators in this way were actually early precursors of the Hollybush quarry or the remains of garden cultivation. The few possible houses outside the gate should be regarded as being extramural to the fort and not as part of a major external settlement.

The hillfort on Midsummer Hill is extremely unusual (if not unique) in encompassing two hills and the dramatic ravine between them. Although, like other hillforts, it has highly visible ramparts, it is nevertheless inward looking, its focal point being the sheltered internal valley and the spring that it harbours. Except possibly at the southern end of Midsummer Hill, there is little indication of chronological overlap among the building stances. The occupation represented by these features might, therefore, have been very short-lived. However, Stanford's excavations indicate that the four-post structures were frequently replaced in the same position, suggesting intense activity and competition for space. The possibility that the house stances were also re-used many times cannot be ignored. The plan so engraved is of a well-established blueprint – the construction of the terraces has determined the form and nature of settlement within the hillfort. No mean effort has been invested in providing level areas for the construction of buildings, although why this was done is less than clear. Many of the slopes are so steep that the structures would be almost unusable in an everyday domestic or agricultural context. Similar observations can be made for platforms within many hillforts.

The nature of the occupation remains uncertain. While many of the stances probably represent domestic use, some are too small and many must have had agricultural or other functions. Stanford interpreted the four-post structures he excavated as a mix of domestic buildings and storehouses (1981; 1988, 26–8). Following Gent (1983) there is a tendency to interpret them all as granaries. However, nine

Fig 2.13
Midsummer Hill.

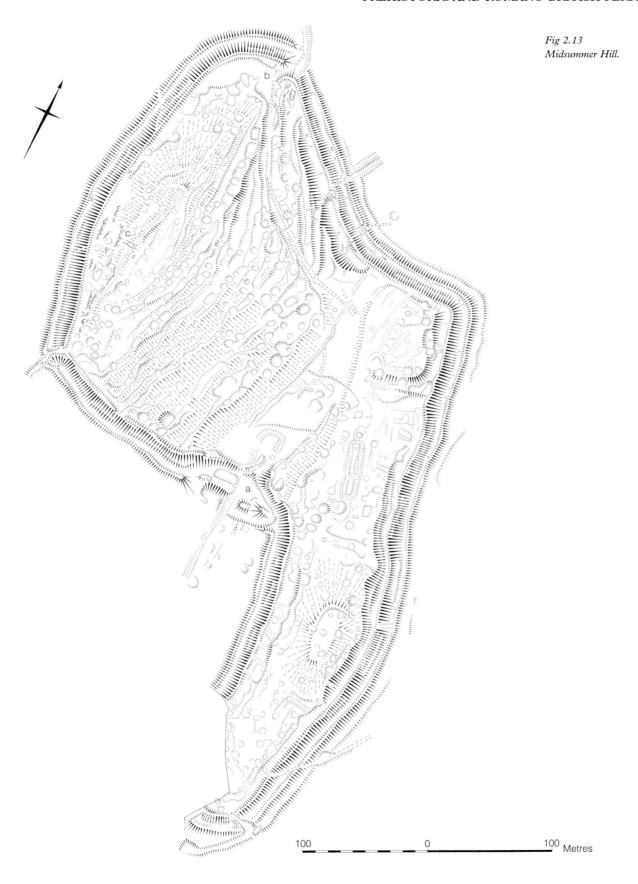

100　　　　0　　　　100 Metres

contained potsherds and three (apparently) hearths, while of thirty-one structures excavated only seven produced evidence of grain. If they were indeed storehouses these four-post structures might well have held chickens, cheese or other produce as well as grain.

Malvern water has been respected as particularly pure during historical times and some springs have been revered and given holy names. The position of the Hollybush spring, hidden in a valley between two striking hills, might only add to its significance in prehistory and enhance the position of the hillfort as a site of symbolic value. The possibly symbolic significance of a natural water source within a hillfort has also been discussed in the case of The Breiddin, Powys (Buckland *et al* 2001).

The use of hillforts

Hillforts are enclosed and defended places but they might also have had many other uses. Their ramparts might have symbolised prestige, power and social inclusion or exclusion. Elements of ritual or ceremony might have been embodied in their design, as in the orientation of their entrances, for instance, or in the use of distinctive stone types in the facing of their ramparts, as at Midsummer Hill. Although nothing is known of the interior arrangements of the smaller hillforts around the Malverns, both British Camp and Midsummer Hill have the remains of substantial numbers of buildings, some of which, at least, were presumably dwellings while others might have served agricultural or other purposes. These could have been large settlements, but the buildings might not all have been in contemporary use. The evidence of frequent re-building at Midsummer Hill suggests that these settlements might have lasted for some time, although not necessarily as long as Dr Stanford postulated.

There remains the question, however, of whether these were permanent, all year round or seasonal settlements. While the Malvern hillforts, like many others in Britain, are in exposed locations there is little doubt that they *could* have been occupied all year round. This does not mean, however, that they *were* and it is possible that they formed part of a transhumant pattern of life – one that was common to many parts of Britain until relatively recently and was certainly practised in this region in the medieval period (*see* Chapter 3). Nevertheless, the apparently large size of the populations in comparison to the relatively restricted amount of upland grazing represented by the narrow range of hills suggests that any such system would not have been built purely on a pragmatic

agricultural basis unless, as Bond suggests (1981, 97), Longdon Marsh was also used for summer grazing. It would be necessary to postulate other, ceremonial or ritual, reasons for a seasonal use of the hills and of these hillforts. On the other hand, the populations of the hillforts might not have been large. Relatively light seasonal, or otherwise interrupted, occupation of a hillfort has recently been suggested at The Breiddin on the basis of environmental evidence (Buckland *et al* 2001).

It has often been assumed that hillforts represent the top level of a hierarchy of Iron Age settlements but the evidence does not necessarily support this view. Hillforts, when excavated, do not produce finds of higher status than other settlement sites, nor are there identifiable 'chiefs' houses' to show a hierarchy *within* the hillforts. It might have been, however, that the hillforts were pre-eminent by reason of their capacity for storing produce, as suggested at Midsummer Hill in the four-post structures, and by the very existence of their ramparts, which took so much labour to build and to maintain.

The relationship of British Camp and Midsummer Hill to each other and to the other neighbouring forts is open to question. Whether they were strictly contemporary is unknown at present, which makes any further discussion on this point almost redundant. However, it is worth noting that 'paired' hillforts are known locally (Jackson 1999, 202, 210) and elsewhere in Britain. It is also notable that within such pairings the forts tend to be of different sizes and forms, and in differing topographical locations.

Whether each hillfort had a distinct territory, as has been argued in the past (eg Cunliffe 1991, 354; Stanford 1980, fig 19), is also open to question. The re-dating of the Shire Ditch and other evidence (*see below*) suggests that the Malvern Hills were a boundary in later prehistory, as they have been in historical times; perhaps the hillforts are on the margins of territories, rather than central to them.

The characterisation of the locations of hillforts as marginal or liminal also recalls the spiritual associations of the Hills, which are more clearly seen in earlier and later periods. (It is interesting to note that among the warlike characters who meet at British Camp in the first scene of Elgar's *Cararctacus* are the 'Spirits of the Hill'.) Like hillforts in Wales, the Cotswold escarpment and elsewhere, British Camp and Midsummer Hill are placed so as to utilise the resources of both the uplands that they occupy and the surrounding lowlands. Like the Cotswold edge hillforts too, which might have been placed to control trade routes along the

Severn and Warwickshire Avon rivers (Sherratt 1996), British Camp and Midsummer Hill might have controlled routes around and across the hills. The positioning of British Camp above Wynds Point and close to the 'Silurian Pass', and Midsummer Hill between Hollybush and The Gullet, supports such an interpretation. However, the cautionary words of Alcock (1965, 184–5) about the extent to which hillforts can be regarded as 'military' must be borne in mind. This is a matter for continuing debate (see, eg Hill 1996 and references therein). British Camp and Midsummer Hill are two very different hillforts: Midsummer Hill quite extraordinary in topography, focused on its ravine and spring – fore-shadowing the importance of water which is an overriding theme in the history of the Malverns; British Camp is more 'typical', more obviously dominant in the landscape. The smaller surrounding hillforts are yet different again. There could hardly be a better illustration of the diversity of hillforts within a small region.

How the hillforts fit into the wider pattern of Iron Age settlement in the area is a still more intractable problem because that wider pattern is at present almost unknown. However, in the lower Severn Valley generally settlement was abundant on the river terraces (T Moore forthcoming a) and this would have been an agriculturally productive area to which the hills might have been symbolically significant, if economically peripheral. The hillforts might have been very different from other contemporary settlement sites – remote retreats that might not have been year-round centres of agricultural production.

Other settlement and activity

Any of the enclosures mentioned in the Bronze Age section above might equally, or more probably, be of Iron Age date. The distribution of these sites, like that of the ring ditches, is very much skewed towards the southern fringes of the project area, just below the 200m contour (see Fig 2.10), which may reflect current land use rather than any real archaeological pattern. One of these enclosures has been excavated, by Herefordshire Archaeology, and demonstrated to belong to the Iron Age. The following account of that site is based on the work of Tim Hoverd (2000b).

Cradley

A rectangular enclosure at the Ridgeway, Cradley (Fig 2.14), found by aerial photography, measures approximately 80m by 60m and is situated on the crest of a ridge. Excavation

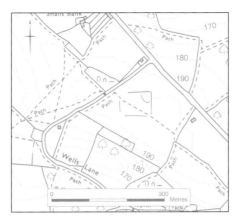

uncovered two truncated pits in the interior, from one of which a fragment of Iron Age pottery was recovered. The enclosing V-shaped ditch, 3m wide, survived to a depth of 2m. This ditch had been deliberately backfilled, first with material from the internal bank, and then with a mix of soil and domestic and 'industrial' waste, including more than 70 sherds of Iron Age pottery. The 'industrial' finds included metal working slag and a fragment of copper alloy. The ditch was then sealed by a working floor, possibly for smelting metal, which showed as a dense spread of ash containing further Iron Age sherds. Here then is an enclosure that might have had agricultural as well as domestic use, but that also certainly had a metalworking application that continued after the enclosing bank and ditch had been levelled.

Elsewhere settlement is suggested by a number of similar enclosures revealed as cropmarks by aerial photography. Five of these are at Donnington and there are others scattered throughout the area (Fig 2.15 shows some examples). These enclosures are likely to be of approximately the same date as Cradley, some time after 400 BC, although the ones at Donnington might be later (see below). There is a pattern of enclosed settlement building across the west midlands in the Middle and Later Iron Age (T Moore forthcoming a).

Russell's End

A different type of site is located close to Russell's End Farm, Bromsberrow (Fig 2.16). This small, triple-ditched, irregular enclosure (SO 73 SW 31) is known only from aerial photographs. It is situated at the north end of a knoll and is now only a few metres south of the M50 motorway. The inner ditch is relatively narrow and might have been a palisade trench but the outer ditches are substantial, up to 4.5m wide. Breaks in these outer ditches might have been a south-facing entrance. The interior

Fig 2.15
Comparative plans of
rectangular enclosures; ***a***
Pendock; ***b*** *Cotheridge;* ***c***
Lowbands; ***d*** *Donnington.*
Although undated, these
are probably of the later
Iron Age. (Based on an
Ordnance Survey map.
© Crown copyright. All
rights reserved. English
Heritage licence no.
100019088.)

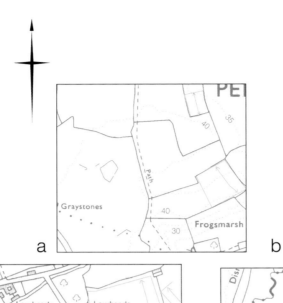

a

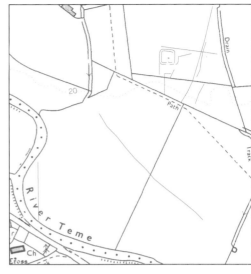

b

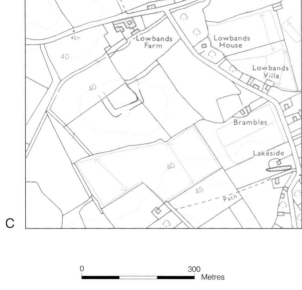

c

d

0 ___ 300
Metres

Fig 2.16
Russell's End enclosure.
This unusual site is
possibly of Iron Age date,
although its origins could
lie in the later Bronze
Age; alternatively, it could
be of post-Roman date
(see Chapter 3). (Based
on an Ordnance Survey
map. © Crown copyright.
All rights reserved.
English Heritage licence
no. 100019088.)

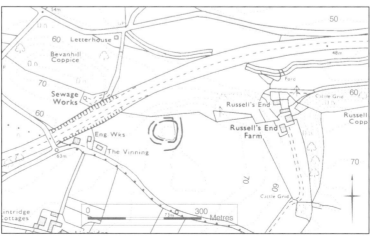

measures less than 50m across and it is therefore too small to be considered as a hillfort although it is likely to have been a substantial settlement of Iron Age date, perhaps with origins in the Later Bronze Age.

Pottery manufacture

It is clear that other activity was taking place around the Malvern area in the Iron Age from at least 400 BC. Quantities of pottery manufactured with inclusions of mineral fragments from the Malvern Hills have been found at a wide range of sites, both locally and regionally. The use of Malvern rock as a temper might have had a symbolic as well as a practical element, if the Hills themselves were regarded as sacred (*see* T Moore forthcoming b). The distribution of the pots suggests well-organised exchange or trade networks involving specialist potters in the Malvern district (Peacock 1968). The existence of pottery manufacture (and metalworking) implies the presence of substantial woodland as a source of fuel. However, the pottery manufacturing sites have yet to be located. Of the three distinct groups of Iron Age pottery made close to the Malverns, one was distributed to the east of the hills and another was confined to the west. Peacock considered that this implies that the hills formed a boundary at this period, perhaps political, although perhaps no more than a demarcation between the 'markets' of different groups of potters (ibid 424). However, this can now be equated with all the other evidence for seeing the Malverns as a symbolic or political boundary at this period.

Deposited items

Other than the above, Iron Age activity is attested only by a handful of findspots, but those finds are of particular interest.

First are two hoards of iron currency bars, found about half a mile or a mile (depending on which authority one follows) north of the Wyche Cutting (*Archaeol J* **14**, 1857, 81–2; R Smith 1905, 183–4; C Smith 1957, 23). The first of these was found in 1856 in one of the 'dingles' on the east side of the hills. The second was found the following year within about 3m of the first. Each contained the remains of about 150 bars, 'which together would be a good load for a mule or a male horse,' as the Reverend F Dyson commented at the time of the second discovery (Allen 1967, 332). Currency bars are rods or bars of metal, often pointed at one end and with some kind of socket, tang or handle at the other. They are an early form of currency and it has been argued that they might also have formed iron stock for the blacksmithing community.

They date from between 300 BC and 1 BC. The Malvern hoards consist of spit-shaped bars, typical in this part of the country.

Hingley has argued (1990) that as well as any utilitarian or currency function, these bars also have a symbolic role inherent in their shapes and in the way in which they were deposited. They are sword-shaped, plough-share-shaped and spit-shaped, but they are not meant to be used as any of these tools because the type of metal is wrong or because the design is exaggerated to the point where the tool could not actually work. Where currency bars are found in settlement contexts they are nearly always located at the boundaries of the settlement. Hingley notes that the full range of types is also found in 'natural' contexts – rivers, lakes, bogs, caves and rocks. The Malvern hoards fall into the latter category. These natural places might also have marked boundaries on a larger scale – between political territories. Once again, therefore, these finds emphasise the role of the Malvern Hills as a boundary in later prehistory.

The other chance finds are of coins, which all date to the Late Iron Age, after about 100 BC. Two have been found at or near Dymock and one near Great Malvern. These three coins constitute almost the total evidence for the Late Iron Age in the area (and one of them might be a curated item from a Roman context). They do not add greatly to our understanding, although it may be significant that they all come from south and east of the Hills.

Discussion

It is possible to see the Malvern area as a frontier zone during the Iron Age, continuing a pattern established in the Later Bronze Age, if not before. In the Iron Age, however, frontiers are marked not by physical linear boundaries but perhaps by the building of hillforts and by the more subtle means of depositing chosen objects in special places. This latter concept implies ceremonial activity, perhaps involving large numbers of people, a forerunner of the beating-of-the-bounds, a significant ceremony recorded in later centuries.

As well as the transition from the Later Bronze Age to the Iron Age there are distinct periods of change within the Iron Age. During the first period, probably about 400 BC, British Camp was enlarged, the rectangular enclosed settlements were created and the Malvern potteries were established. The growth of a regionally significant ceramics industry, replacing local pottery manufacture, might have been mirrored in a general move back to the use of long-distance exchange systems that had been a feature of earlier periods. The second transition, at about 100 BC, is not marked in the Malverns as there is hardly any evidence that can be dated to the Late Iron Age. This in itself may be significant, however, if it marks a shift in settlement patterns.

These transitions must be due to radical changes in perceptions of the organisation of settlement space and of the landscape, reflecting transformations in society itself. These might have involved ideas about community, kinship, households, social stratification and land tenure (T Moore forthcoming a). The lack of obviously high-status dwellings, in hillforts and elsewhere, brings into question the whole structure of Early Iron Age society. While at the end of the period, after about 100 BC, there is a well-known hierarchy of farmers, warriors, druids, chiefs and even kings in southern Britain – attested both by archaeological and written evidence – it is not clear that this is an evolutionary development from what had gone before or something entirely novel. Earlier Iron Age society might have been less deeply hierarchical. One possible model suggests that leadership might have been exercised by fluid groups of 'elders', people whose age, experience or particular abilities set them above their fellows, but whose authority was not hereditary.

The Roman period (AD 43–400)

The impact made by the Claudian invasion of AD 43 on the Malvern region was probably profound, but might not have been as sudden as is generally assumed. Aspects of Roman culture had been creeping into southern Britain for more than 100 years and in some parts of the south-east, at least, the invasion was only a culminating act in the process of 'becoming Roman' of the leaders of society. In the south-west there was more resistance to the invaders. However, the apparent absence of Roman military sites around the Malverns, especially when contrasted with the rash of early forts in the territory of the Silures to the west, suggests that the local population – part of the tribal grouping known as the Dobunni – was generally pro-Roman (Millett 1990, 42–55). There is almost no evidence for the Late Iron Age and little more for the early Roman period. Such evidence as there is largely concerns one aspect of the economic life of the district – pottery manufacture.

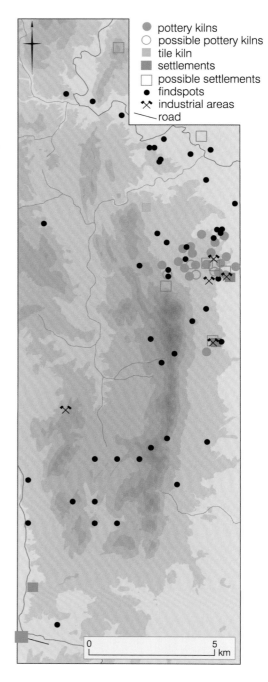

pottery kilns
possible pottery kilns
tile kiln
settlements
possible settlements
findspots
industrial areas
road

0   5 km

The Iron Age potteries, which had flourished since the 4th century BC, received a boost at the time of the invasion, perhaps driven by demand from the Roman military (Millett 1990, 56), and perhaps because pottery was now seen as a necessary adjunct to 'romanized' life, in a way that it had not been before. At least twenty individual pottery kiln sites are known (Fig 2.17), although no intact kiln structure has yet been found. The industry spans the whole of the Roman period, from the mid-1st century to the

4th (Peacock 1967; Swan 1984 F 352, 673–6). The evidence consists for the most part of concentrations of pot fragments, including wasters (mis-shapen vessels) and underfired vessels. In a few cases there is kiln furniture and debris. In one case, at Great Buckman's Farm (Waters 1976), traces of a possible timber building were found and at Marley Hall near Ledbury (outside the Project area) there were other traces of infrastructure (Watkins 1932). These included a stone-lined culvert leading from an adjacent spring and a paved roadway, as well as deposits of washed but unused clay.

Most of the well-documented examples lie to the east of the hills, though there are possible kiln sites to the west, including the one at Marley Hall. Fieldwork for the current project has identified other possible kilns on Oyster Hill (Hoverd 2003, 26–7), although what the product of these might have been is unclear. All the kilns to the east of the hills are situated on the Mercia Mudstone and all are within a short distance of streams.

Fuel is the other vital requirement and the existence of such a significant and long-lived industry demands a renewable energy resource. This implies that coppiced woodland would have been a significant part of the landscape throughout the Roman period and probably back into the Iron Age. The Malvern potteries were making a wide range of goods including cooking pots, various forms of bowls and jars, dishes, flagons and tankards. They might even

have been making some colanders and mortaria (gritted mixing bowls). The products of these kilns are distributed as widely as their Iron Age forerunners, except that they are not found around Gloucester and on the Cotswolds – other kilns had taken that market. They are found both on military and on civilian sites, and in the 2nd century tankards and jars made at these kilns or others producing 'Severn Valley Wares' reached Hadrian's Wall (P Webster 1976). Tiles were also made in the area during the 2nd century and a kiln for this purpose has been excavated at Leigh Sinton (Waters 1963).

With the exception of a possible early fort at Dymock (Leech 1981, 30), for which the evidence is not strong, there is no trace of Roman military activity in the area. The placing of Caractacus' last stand against the legions at British Camp is fanciful, although there is a small Roman fort, probably of rather later date, at Tedstone Wafer (G Webster 1954), beyond the north-western limit of the study area. Evidence for civil settlement and industrial (mainly metalworking) activity, on the other hand, has been found at about twelve locations within the project area (*see* Fig 2.17), some of them adjacent to pottery kilns. (The exact number of industrial sites is ambiguous because we cannot be certain whether or not some records refer to the same sites.) The most extensive known settlement is that at Dymock, which has been equated with the 'Macatonion' of the *Ravenna Cosmography* (Leech 1981, 30–1; McWhirr 1981, 67–70). This is a 'ribbon development' along the Roman road from Gloucester to Stretton Grandison. Building foundations, ditches, rubbish pits, road surfaces and a whole range of objects have been discovered, indicating intensive occupation in the 3rd and 4th centuries, possibly arising out of the presence of the postulated earlier fort on the site. Other potentially interesting sites are at The Greenway, Donnington (Jack 1914a, 69; 1914b, 108), North End Farm (*Britannia* **26**, 1995, 352) and The Chase High School/DERA site (Griffin *et al* 2000, 6–7, 11). It has been suggested that the group of enclosures seen as cropmarks at Donnington may be of Roman date because of the numbers of finds of Romano-British material from this area (Keith Ray pers comm). The pottery industry presumably generated some wealth but there is no evidence for its use. Dymock is the only settlement that has any pretensions to urban status. Villas are almost entirely restricted to the south-eastern half of Dobunnic territory, beyond the River Severn, and nothing of that description has yet been found near the Malverns. The recent discovery of a fragment of a Venus figurine (Fig 2.18) near

Fig 2.18
Fragment of a Venus figurine found near one of the Roman pottery production sites; is it of Roman date or a later copy? (height of surviving fragment = 32mm; private collection)

Fig 2.19
Coppiced woodland would certainly have been as much a feature of the Roman – and even earlier – landscape around the Malverns as it has been of later ones.

one of the pottery production sites, may indicate the site of high-status Roman activity. However, the specialists are currently undecided as to whether this is a genuine Roman artefact or a Victorian copy (Derek Hurst pers comm).

Beyond the settlement sites there are widespread indications of activity across the landscape throughout the Roman period (*see* Fig 2.17), consisting mainly of finds of pottery, with the occasional coin or piece of personal jewellery. Deposits of special objects were still being made in Roman Britain and shortly after the beginning of the 4th century someone buried a hoard of about 300 coins on the Hills some distance to the north-east of British Camp (Robertson 2000, 238). The remote and rocky location, like that of the Iron Age currency bars, suggests a religious or ceremonial motivation.

The picture that emerges of the Malvern area in the Roman period is one of a widely-settled and, in places, intensively-industrialised landscape. The industries, however, were ones that relied on the local natural resources of minerals and water, and on the provision of extensive well-managed woodland (Fig 2.19).

3

The medieval and later periods

The medieval period starts with the end of formal Roman rule in Britain in the 5th century and ends, for the purposes of this book, with the suppression of the monasteries at the hands of King Henry VIII in the later 1530s. We have placed the division of 'early' and 'high' periods at the Domesday survey of 1086, rather than the actual Norman Conquest twenty years earlier, as this is probably a more significant event for landscape history and archaeology.

Early medieval (*c* 400–1086)

If the evidence for activity around the Malverns in the prehistoric and Roman periods is thinner than is desirable, for the early medieval period it is almost non-existent. This may not be really true, of course. Evidence is probably there. The problem is that the skills to recognise it have not yet been developed. From an archaeologist's perspective, one of the main problems is that pottery ceases to be manufactured or used in this area (Gelling 1992, 179–80) and one of the principal chronological and economic 'markers' is therefore lost. It also seems that across England neither the indigenous population at this time nor the Anglo-Saxon incomers was concerned to transform the landscape with earthworks and other large structures – excepting the truly massive but rare boundary works such as Offa's Dyke. Certainly it is not easily possible to recognise many landscape features as being distinctly early medieval in date.

Another local difficulty is in finding the population; the distinctive 'pagan Anglo-Saxon' burials, from which so much knowledge of early Saxon England derives, are not found to the west of Worcester. Place-name evidence suggests a continuing strong British presence in the lower Severn Valley and it might have been that the strength of a 'Celtic' Christian community in this area halted the advance of the pagan Anglo-Saxons initially (Hooke 1985, 4, 9–10). In Herefordshire too, place name evidence suggests that much of the county was at least partly Welsh-speaking until, or even beyond, the

Norman Conquest in 1066 (Gelling 1992, 69-70, 100). It is possible, as has been argued elsewhere (eg Eagles 2001), that the framework of the Roman *civitates* (local authorities) may have continued for some time after the official end of Roman rule.

The documents reveal that the Malverns were, once again, a border area in the early medieval period. From the early 7th century at least, the ridge of the hills formed part of the boundary between the Hwicce (Hooke 1985), to the east, and the Magonsaetan (Gelling 1992, 80–3 et passim), to the west. These were two closely-allied subordinate kingdoms, probably of mixed British and Anglian peoples, founded by the Mercians as buffer zones against the Welsh and the West Saxons (and occupying a remarkably similar territory to the Dobunni five hundred years before). When the sees of Hereford and Worcester were created, following the conversion of Mercia to Christianity in the later 7th century, they adopted the same boundary (and the bishops of Worcester continued to call themselves 'Bishops of the Hwicce' until the 10th century). The Malvern ridge seems to have formed an estate boundary by the 10th century (Hooke 1990, 215).

Despite the occurrence of plagues and economic collapse, it is inherently unlikely that an apparently vigorous Romano-British population simply disappeared and left the area unpopulated in the 5th century. The general lack of physical evidence from this period in many regions led landscape historians to suggest that the incoming Anglo-Saxons found a deserted wildwood. It has been demonstrated that this is not the case, that the British population is archaeologically difficult to see rather than absent (eg Bassett 2000). Nevertheless, in looking at the immediate environs of the Malverns – especially Longdon Marsh, the moors of Castlemorton and Birtsmorton – it is possible to speculate that much of this area might have been uncultivated and well wooded during the early medieval period. Place names, especially incorporating the element 'leah', suggest as much for large parts of western Worcestershire at this time.

This evidence does not suggest under-use, however. Woodland resources are valuable and not available in more intensively cultivated areas. Swine pasture at Leigh Sinton was the subject of dispute in 825. There are clear linkages between estates to the east in the cultivated Severn and Avon valleys and those in the woodland zones, which may have provided them with summer pastures and autumn pannage (pasture for pigs) as well as timber (Hooke 1985, 180–5, fig 42, et passim). This is certainly true of Welland, Redmarley, Leigh, Longdon, Eldersfield, Berrow and Pendock (Bond 1981, 97–8; Dyer 1990, 104-5). These links are accentuated in the landscape by broad drove roads, such as the one that now, in part, forms the main street of Castlemorton.

As in prehistoric periods, but now with firm documentary evidence, it can be said that the Malvern Hills and their surrounding areas formed part of a system of linked estates that might have developed from a system of transhumance. To the west of the hills, meanwhile, there are almost no 'leah' names and the Domesday survey suggests a much less wooded landscape (Gelling 1992, 16, fig 7). Why this should be, and how much reliance can be placed on this negative evidence, is uncertain. (It may be significant that two of the 'leah' names that *do* exist to the west of the Hills, Cowleigh and Farley, were within Mathon parish, the only part of Worcestershire to extend west of the ridge.) The Hills themselves, however, might have been largely deserted. The foundation stories of Great Malvern Priory tell of the wild and uncultivated nature of the Hills – a fit landscape for holy men and hermits to fight the good fight. Although these stories may be to some extent fabrications of the later medieval period, they may contain an element of truth.

Physical remains of this period in the landscape are hard to find. Few of the hedges noted in pre-Norman Conquest charters have survived (Hooke 1985, 240). Some roads dating to this period still survive in places. Charters of the 10th and 11th centuries, for example, mention 'Suþ stræte' (ibid, 120, fig 30), which came west from Worcester along what is now the B4485, through Rushwick and crossed the River Teme at Bransford Bridge, then continued along the line of the Suckley Road. None of the churches in the area has any definitely Anglo-Saxon fabric, although St Michael's, Ledbury is on the site of a minster probably founded in the 8th century (Hillaby 1997, 1) and St Mary's, Dymock has very 'early Norman' features that might be of pre-Norman Conquest date (Fig 3.1). Keith Ray and Tim Hoverd have recently drawn attention to surviving fragments of early medieval sculpture within Cradley church (*West Midlands Archaeol* **43**, 2000, 56). It has been suggested that Dymock was continuously settled from the Romano-British period onwards (Leech 1981, 31) but no firm evidence of early medieval occupation has yet been found. The Domesday survey makes reference to certain occupied places, such as Bagburrow and Colwall, but although these names still exist there is no indication of where precisely these settlements were in the 11th century. Charter references to 'haga' enclosures imply that deer hunting was a significant activity around the hills before the Norman Conquest (Hooke 1985, 185), as it was to be afterwards.

Of the undated field monuments, either earthworks or cropmark sites, some *might* be of early medieval date. The enclosure at Russell's End (*see* Fig 2.16) is one such possibility, not because it looks like any known early medieval site but because it does not look particularly like a site of any other date.

Fig 3.1
St Mary's Church, Dymock. The blind arcading is one of several features suggesting a mid to late 11th –century date for the church, but Dymock might have been a centre of Christianity much earlier than this. (Photographed by F E Howard of the National Buildings Record in 1922.)

The high medieval period (1086–1539)

This period has left a rich legacy in hamlets, farmsteads, churches, castles, moats and landscape features of many types. For the first time in the Malvern area there is a wealth of physical evidence (Fig 3.2).

Secular power

One of the few archaeologically recognisable results of the Norman conquest of England was the construction of castles, as a distinct new type of fortified lordly residence expressing the new secular power. There are three castles on and around the Malverns – at Castlemorton, at Castle Green (Leigh) and at Herefordshire Beacon. All three are small, but none the less interesting for that. For much of the medieval period the real centre of secular power to the east of the Hills lay at Hanley Castle (Hurle 1978; Toomey 2001), a property of the Earls of Gloucester. To the west the Bishops of Hereford held sway; they owned every Herefordshire manor adjoining the Hills. There were, however, numerous other landholders of greater or lesser account, including the two monastic houses located within the region and others without.

Castlemorton

Immediately to the south of Castlemorton church are the earthwork remains of a castle (NMR SO 73 NE 4; Fig 3.3). The dominant feature is an oval motte or mound, now much overgrown. A surrounding ditch with counterscarp bank survives on the southern side and there are traces of subsidiary enclosures to the east and north, although whether these are part of the castle or part of the medieval and later settlement of Castlemorton is not clear. A series of depressions stretching away to the south have been described as fishponds, though it is interesting to note that the *Victoria County History* (VCH 1924, 426) refers to them as 'irregular clay-pits'. The secondary use of clay pits as ponds is a possibility. The castle was built probably before the end of the 12th century (Allen Brown 1989, 106) by the Foliot family – the place was at one time known as Morton Foliot. The VCH (1924, 49) suggests that it was built during the 'Anarchy' of King Stephen's reign (1139–53). It is common to ascribe castle-building to particular periods of strife, but castles are lordly residences and administrative centres, not just forts, and it is not necessary to find a military context for the

creation of a castle. The Foliots sold Castlemorton to Richard de Berkyng, Abbot of Westminster (1222–46), who appointed a chaplain to celebrate mass daily in the castle chapel (ibid, 49–50).

This evidence raises some questions. Why did the Abbot of Westminster want this castle, and why the insistence on a daily mass? Was the 'chapel in the castle' a building now lost or was it St Gregory's? St Gregory's is now (since 1880) the parish church, but it was originally a Norman chapel (ibid, 51) and the enclosures to

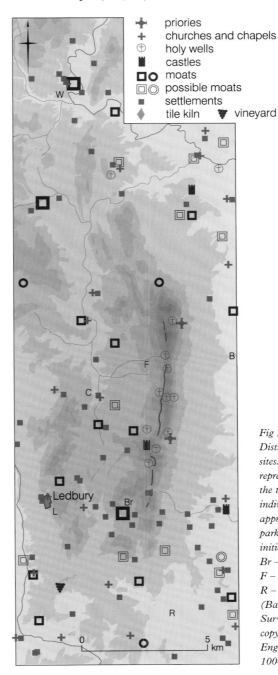

Fig 3.2
Distribution map of medieval sites. The settlement symbols represent a range of sites from the town of Ledbury down to individual dwellings. The approximate positions of the parks are marked by their initial letters: B – Blackmore; Br – Bronsil; C – Colwall; F – Farley; L – Ledbury; R – Redmarley; W – Whitbourne. (Based on an Ordnance Survey map. © Crown copyright. All rights reserved. English Heritage licence no. 100019088.)

Fig 3.3

Plan of the castle at Castlemorton, based on an OS Antiquity Model (NMR SO 73 NE 4) with additions. (Antiquity Models were drawings by OS Archaeology Division Field Investigators indicating changes to the depiction of antiquities on new editions of OS maps. They were prepared on small extracts cut from old, pre-national grid maps.)

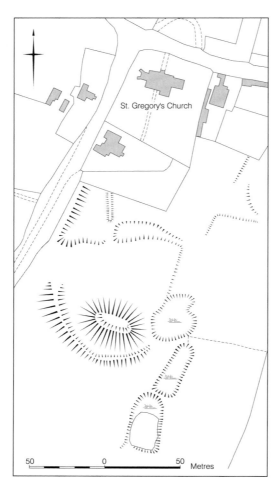

Fig 3.4

Plan of the castle at Castle Green, Leigh, based on an OS Antiquity Model (NMR SO 75 SE 4).

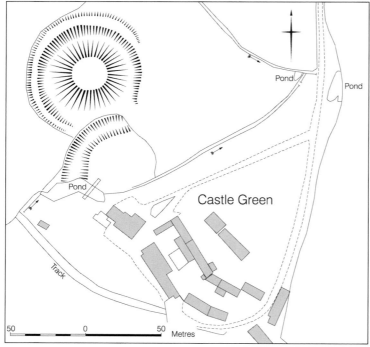

the north of the castle might have encompassed it. The Abbot's interest is probably to be explained in terms of the dispute between Westminster and Worcester over Great Malvern Priory (*see below*). The castle at Castlemorton was possibly the closest lordly residence to that monastery that the Abbot could get his hands on, although Westminster Abbey had considerable estates elsewhere in Worcestershire (Bond 1988, 127). The daily mass might have been arranged for the religious edification of the local peasantry (although they would have been obliged to attend their parish church at Longdon), but is much more likely to have been an expression – deliberately provocative maybe – of the Abbot's temporal rights, in this frontierland so far from Westminster and so close to the rival's headquarters. The abbots of Westminster seem to have seen Great Malvern Priory itself as a stronghold in the midst of the diocese of Worcester (Hooke 1985, 182).

Castle Green, Leigh

There is a large, though not particularly high, motte with a shallow ditch and broad counterscarp bank at Castle Green (Fig 3.4). Some water features (apparently much altered) survive to the south, although whether they represent a bailey, as has been suggested (VCH 1924, 426), is not clear. There is no visible trace of enclosures farther to the south and east among the farm buildings and a large, recently-dug fishing pond to the east now occupies much of what was probably once a bailey. The ground to the west is under arable and ploughing has encroached on the outer edge of the counterscarp bank. The motte itself is suffering damage by burrowing animals. The manor of Castle Leigh was held by the Pembridges from the abbots of Pershore in the 13th century and it has been suggested that the castle was built by Henry de Pembridge during the Baron's War (1263–7), in which conflict he was active (ibid, 102).

As noted above, it is not necessary to find a military reason for the creation of a castle. Nevertheless, it is of some interest that this castle was built within what seems to have been a rather minor subordinate manor and a primarily military origin might have been the case here.

Herefordshire Beacon and the Shire Ditch

The ringwork crowning Herefordshire Beacon is in a distinctly different topographical location (Fig 3.5). Although superficially it is of the same general 'class' of monument as the other two castles, its location shows that it was built for very different reasons. While Castlemorton and Castle Green belong to the settled woodland landscape, this ringwork belongs to the wild, liminal landscape of the Hills. It consists of a rock-cut ditch of ovoid plan surrounding a disturbed platform, and a counterscarp platform of widely varying width (*see* Fig 2.12), possibly forming a small, attenuated bailey, to the east (King and Alcock 1969, 97, 116; Bowden 2000a, 9–10, 14–16). The spoil from the massive flat-bottomed ditch has been used both to level up the interior and to create the large counterscarp bank externally. This substantial feat of earth and rock moving has transformed the summit from its natural, conical form to a 'pill-box' shape. There are two causeways across the ditch, the southern one being original, the other perhaps a secondary construction. The interior of the ringwork is a platform surrounded by a rampart, substantial on the south and east, slighter on the north and absent to the west. Internal features are difficult to interpret. Some might mark the sites of small towers or other medieval buildings while others could represent later activity, including the excavations of 1879 (Hilton Price 1887).

Within the bailey formed by the counterscarp is a rectangular building platform (*see* Fig 2.12 **g**) and some other scarps. Further scarping below at **h** and **j** appears to be recent but may be of medieval date. The two scarps at **h**, forming a possible building platform, continue the alignment of the northern side of the counterscarp and might have been intended to control access to the secondary north-eastern entrance.

The ringwork is morphologically of medieval date, but the chronology of mottes and ringworks is now known to be more extended than was once thought. It might, therefore, have been built at any time between the Norman Conquest and the 14th century, though a date between the late 11th century and the end of the 12th century is most likely. Unfortunately the results of the 1879 excavations do not throw any light on this question.

The relationship of this castle to the Shire Ditch is of crucial importance (Fig 3.6). The traditional history of the Shire Ditch is that it was created by Gilbert de Clare, Earl of Gloucester, in about 1287 as the result of a dispute with Thomas de Cantilupe, Bishop of Hereford. About three years previously, the Earl had appropriated land in Colwall and Eastnor to his (Malvern) Chase. The ensuing court case was a victory for the Bishop. Legend attaching to this history suggests that the Earl cunningly built

the Ditch on the eastern side of the ridge in the form of a park pale so that deer could leap from the Bishop's land into his but not vice versa. However, it seems clear that the Malvern ridge was a boundary of long standing and that the ditch itself was – in part at least – of prehistoric origin (*see* Chapter 2), so the Earl was (wittingly or unwittingly) re-making an existing boundary. Within this new chronological scheme the stories of the ringwork and the Shire Ditch can be connected. The location of this castle, on a high hilltop remote from contemporary settlement, is rare but not unique; King and Alcock list eight ringworks (including British Camp) 'in lofty hill-top positions' (1969, 102n). It has been suggested that the castle within British Camp was a hunting lodge, built in connection with the establishment of Malvern Chase (Higham and Barker 1992, 200, 239), and there seems to be some merit in this suggestion. Alternatively, or additionally,

Fig 3.5
The ringwork on Herefordshire Beacon, from the south, showing the distinctive shape given to the hill by the medieval earthworks.

Fig 3.6
The Shire Ditch and the ringwork on Herefordshire Beacon. The post-medieval enclosure in a saddle on the edge of Hangman's Hill can also be seen, bottom right. (Aerial photograph by Harold Wingham, August 1958.)

it seems possible that the castle owes its location to the existence of the boundary, perhaps long disputed, marked by the Shire Ditch. Whether its purpose in relation to this boundary was functional or symbolic, or a combination of the two, is of some interest.

The ringwork is relatively small and its attached platform 'bailey' is tiny. By analogy with other sites the whole hillfort should possibly be regarded as the bailey, but even then there is no convincing evidence for medieval building activity. The castle was not, it would seem, established as the base for a substantial permanent garrison that could control the surrounding area and communication routes, nor does it seem well placed to act as a defended residence or a refuge, for it is too far from contemporary centres of settlement. It might, nevertheless, have formed a useful and well-defended look-out post. What is clear, however, is that the ringwork is an outstandingly

prominent feature in the landscape, being visible for miles even today. With a timber tower on top it would have been more prominent still. If it was intended as a symbol of lordship it was a very successful one. Furthermore, it would not be stretching the evidence too far to see this castle acting as a focal point for any ceremonies – in the nature of 'beating the bounds' – connected with the Shire Ditch, rather as Guarlford Court was the resting place during the two-day perambulation of the Chase boundaries in 1584 (B Smith 1978, 27–9).

The symbol of lordship does not only subsist in the prominence of the ringwork, but also in its location within an ancient defended enclosure, which might have been adopted as the bailey and which might have been seen as legitimatising a claim to power, or evoking legends of the past (Coulson 1979, 74). A similar case has been argued, for instance, in somewhat different circumstances for the motte at Thetford, which also lies within an Iron Age enclosure (Everson and Jecock 1999, 105). Placement of early castles within prehistoric enclosures is a widespread phenomenon. In some cases at least, symbolism would seem to have been a consideration in the choice of location. However, such symbolic aspects, whether vested in a motte, ringwork or great tower, do not preclude simultaneous practical functions.

Parks

Another aspect of the expression of power in the landscape is the creation of deer parks. Much of the area to the east of the Hills was under forest law from the late 11th century and became a Chase in 1217, while to the west was the Bishop of Hereford's Chase. Within these hunting areas were parks, successors to the pre-Norman Conquest 'haga', for the breeding and management of deer. Few traces of these have survived into the modern landscape, but the outline of Redmarley d'Abitot park is very clearly seen in current field boundaries to the north-east of Park Farm, sliced in half by the M50 motorway. Others are remembered in place names, such as Blackmore Park and Cowleigh Park Farm – though this one was of post-medieval date (Goodbury 1999, KA). There were others at Farley (a manor within the parish of Mathon) on the south-western slopes of the Worcestershire Beacon, at Colwall, at Ledbury and at Bronsil (Goodbury 1999; B Smith 1978, fig 2; N Smith 2001, 3). The bishops of Hereford

are said to have had a palace (although perhaps hunting lodge would be a more accurate term) at Colwall on or near the present Park Farm, and there are a number of 'park' field names in this locality (Goodbury 1999, IC-IN).

Settlement and agriculture

The Malvern Hills were still regarded as a 'wilderness' in the 12th century, according to William of Malmesbury (Hooke 1985, 180; B Smith 1978, 14). Shortly after the Norman Conquest much of the area came under forest law and remained a chase until the 17th century. However, monastic just-so stories and the reputation of forest law should not overshadow the evidence of a peopled, working landscape on the lower ground, to either side of the ridge. Just over the Hills from the priories was the flourishing borough of Ledbury and numerous rural settlements. While a large part of the area now covered by the town of Great Malvern might have been uninhabited, there was nevertheless abundant settlement and activity not far away, dispersed through the landscape (Hooke 1985, 183).

Change through the medieval period was profound. In his seminal work on Pendock, Dyer (1990) describes a heavily wooded landscape in the 11th century that was cleared and cultivated in the 12th and 13th centuries to such an extent that, having been a dependent specialist

Fig 3.7
Settlement remains and other earthworks at Wayend Street, Eastnor, suggest assarting; the place name with its double suffixes, 'end' and 'street' also suggests late colonisation in at least two phases.

woodland of Overbury, by the 15th century it required its own dependent woodland, at Pendock Grove in Eastnor. The numerous 'End' and 'Street' place names (Fig 3.7) also suggest 13th- or 14th-century colonisation of areas of common wood and waste (Roberts and Wrathmell 2002, 54–6). 'Feld' place names may tell much the same story (Hooke 1985, 184).

Settlement

Ledbury (Fig 3.8) began as a Christian centre with a minster church in the early medieval period. By the time of Domesday it was still a village centred probably on the triangular green, now infilled, immediately to the north-west of the churchyard. The new borough was laid out by Richard de Capella, Bishop of Hereford, starting probably in 1125 (Hillaby 1997, 12–13). The layout of the borough around its market place and its subsequent rapid growth is still clearly marked in the town plan and has been traced in some detail by Hillaby (ibid, 24–30).

With the exception of Pendock and its surrounding area (Bond 1981,100–3, fig 3; Dyer 1990), medieval rural settlement around the hills has not been studied in depth. It is clear, however, that the pattern is of dispersed dwellings and that the few nucleated villages are perhaps rather late developments. Although Bond argued that Castlemorton was once nucleated but began to disperse at an early period (1981, 101), the evidence for nucleation – the earthwork enclosures near church and castle – is open to other interpretations, while the evidence for early dispersal – a string of cruck-built houses extending to the west – is not. At Pendock, Dyer recognised what he called the 'interrupted row' settlement – a network of sunken, hedged lanes with houses at intervals divided by their own small plots (1990, 108–11). It is now clear, especially from the aerial and woodland surveys, that similar arrangements characterised much of the area, indicating a 'typical' woodland settlement pattern.

Fig 3.8
Ledbury. Aerial photograph showing part of the densely packed medieval core of the town, the church and the market place. The earlier triangular green, infilled with buildings, is clearly visible to the left of the church. (Aerial photograph by Chris Musson, August 2000. © Woolhope Naturalists Field Club.)

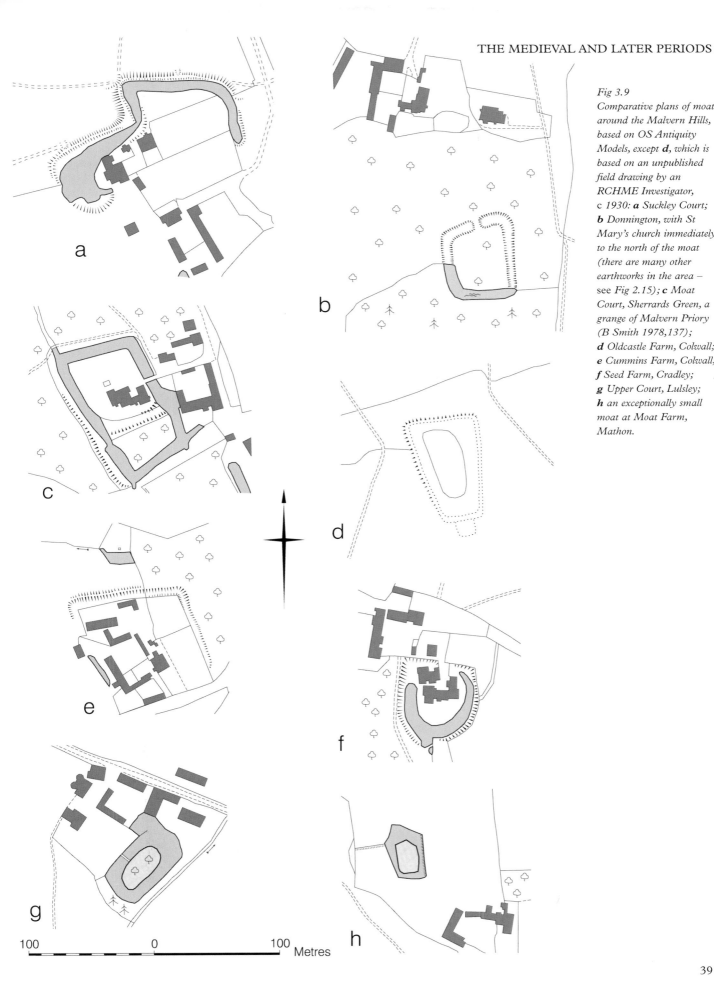

*Fig 3.9
Comparative plans of moats
around the Malvern Hills,
based on OS Antiquity
Models, except **d**, which is
based on an unpublished
field drawing by an
RCHME Investigator,
c 1930: **a** Suckley Court;
b Donnington, with St
Mary's church immediately
to the north of the moat
(there are many other
earthworks in the area –
see Fig 2.15); **c** Moat
Court, Sherrards Green, a
grange of Malvern Priory
(B Smith 1978,137);
d Oldcastle Farm, Colwall;
e Cummins Farm, Colwall;
f Seed Farm, Cradley;
g Upper Court, Lulsley;
h an exceptionally small
moat at Moat Farm,
Mathon.*

100   0   100 Metres

Fig 3.10
Plan of Bronsil Castle.

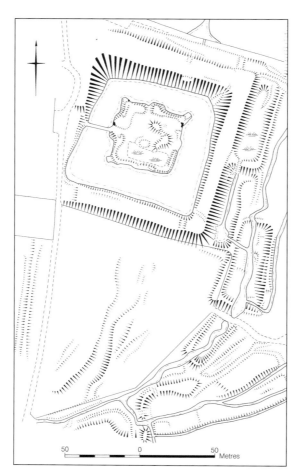

50 0 50
Metres

Much encroachment into woodland or common land, some of it probably of medieval date, has been noted, as at Ravenshill and Coneygore, Alfrick. This is characterised by thinly-dispersed, small farmsteads or cottages occupying sheltered locations with access – often by deep hollow-ways – to adjacent pasture and former arable, orchards, quarries and larger settlements (Mindykowski and Bretherton 2003, 8). A good example is a farmstead to the east of Bradlow Knoll, in Frith Wood (Hoverd 2003, 28–9, 35). This 'woodland' pattern is also represented in the proliferation of moated sites in the area. Bond noted that the moats of Worcestershire are found mainly on the Mercia Mudstone and Lower Lias, but concluded that the more meaningful relationship was with the Forest of Feckenham and Malvern Chase (1978, 71).

Moats are often thought of as being high status sites – manor houses and other aristocratic dwellings. While there is no doubt that the provision of a moat around a house makes a claim for status, that status can be at a relatively low level in the social scale (Fig 3.9). In the Malvern area, with a few notable exceptions (eg Fig 3.9 **a** and **c**), the moats are small and in peripheral locations, close to parish boundaries and often on heavy soils. This echoes Bond's findings for Worcestershire as a whole, where isolated moats far outnumber those in villages or hamlets (ibid. 73). The moat at Upper Court, Lulsley (Fig 3.9 **g**), is fairly typical. The island

Fig 3.11
Bronsil Castle, showing the remaining fragment of one of the gatehouse towers.

itself is small and the moat relatively broad. It lies in a restricted valley just where it opens out onto the floodplain of the River Teme but the location is cramped and essentially north-facing. The main approaches to Upper Court are deeply hollowed. This is not a high-status site, but probably represents colonisation into woodland – in an area where there is as yet no evidence of previous occupation – in the 12th or 13th century, by someone of relatively humble background. The moat would provide a measure of security and a very necessary drainage system as well as being a sign of social pretension. At the other end of the social scale is the large moat at Whitbourne just upstream from Lulsley, which housed one of the Bishop of Hereford's palaces.

However, one of the most informative of the higher-status moated sites is at Bronsil, Eastnor (N Smith 2001; Fig 3.10). Here Richard, Lord Beauchamp, built in the mid-15th century a quadrangular house grand enough to be called a 'Castle'. The house itself was largely demolished and the stone probably re-used in Eastnor Castle in the 19th century, but some masonry and earthworks remain, including one – much re-built – fragment of the gatehouse (Fig 3.11). The surrounding moat is still water-filled and there are other traces of the medieval setting. What seems to be indicated by the earthworks of the moat and a series of ponds to the east, is that Beauchamp's grand house was built on a pre-existing moated site. This might have been a hunting lodge associated with the Bishop of Hereford's Chase.

There was a decline in moat building in the 13th and 14th centuries but thereafter new moats were built and old ones adapted for very different, often ornamental, roles. Bronsil possibly represents just such a re-modelling. Lord Beauchamp was a courtier of King Edward IV and his showpiece 'castle' seems to have been surrounded by elaborate water gardens of a type that has only recently been recognised (Everson 1998).

More unusual moated sites are also found. At Moat Meadow, Eastnor, is a complex site with two moats, one cutting through the other on a different alignment (Fig 3.12). They are on the lip of a west-facing slope above the Glynch Brook, an unusual location, and the flooding of the moats has entailed an elaborate system of leats, although this is probably a later modification. To the south and east of the moats are numerous earthworks, some apparently building platforms. While there is some sign of building on the southernmost (earlier) moat, there is none on the later one. At Redmarley d'Abitot is a circular moat (Wootton and Bowden 2002; Fig 3.13) on an east-facing

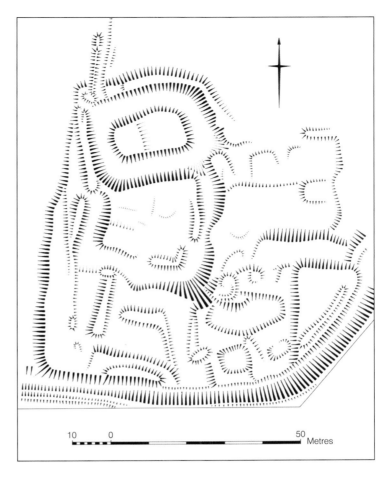

slope. There are traces of buildings on the moat island and externally. Circular moats are rare but not unknown. There is another one within the project area at Seed Farm, Cradley, (see Fig 3.9 f) and there was possibly a third at Cowleigh Park Farm. A strange facet of the Redmarley site, however, is that it appears to have gone unnoticed until the 1970s. This makes one wary of accepting the site as a genuine moat, except that the moats at Moat Meadow, which do seem to be genuine, were not recorded until the 1980s, despite the field name (NMR SO 73 NW 61).

Agriculture and the working landscape

For a nominally 'woodland' area, much of it devoted in the medieval period to hunting and pannage, the region around the Malverns displays a considerable amount of evidence for agriculture in the form of ridge-and-furrow and cultivation terraces (Fig 3.14). However, the plots of ridge-and-furrow tend to be small, which is a typical feature of assarting. Many of them, moreover, are clearly of a late date and can be related to relatively recent orchard planting.

Fig 3.12
Plan of the moats and some of the other earthworks at Moat Meadow, Eastnor.

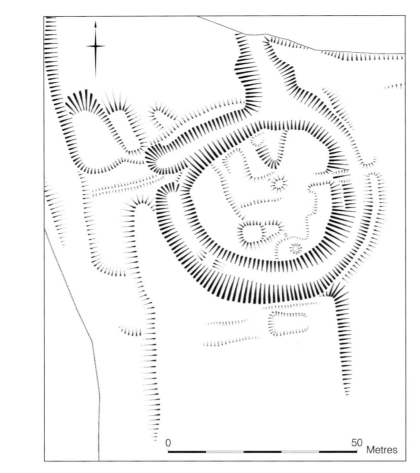

There are instances, nevertheless, where a probable medieval date for ridge-and-furrow cultivation can be demonstrated. The form of ridge-and-furrow around Birts Street and Rye Street strongly suggests medieval cultivation (Fig 3.15). To the south of the Leigh Brook between Leigh and Smith End Green are two plots of slightly curved ridge-and-furrow divided by a headland, which are overlain by the present field boundary – a thorn hedge (NMR SO 75 SE 46).

Of particular significance is the number of occasions on which the woodland survey has found evidence of cultivation under woodland that is now regarded as 'ancient'. In Frith Wood, Ledbury, and on Crews Hill, Suckley, there are massive strip lynchets, terraces formed probably for arable cultivation, although possibly for horticulture. Pottery of 14th-century date has been recovered from the lynchets in Frith Wood. One of the lynchets at Crews Hill is topped by small-leaved lime pollards possibly as much as 600 years old. These represent a boundary established when these fields were turned over to pasture and the formation of the massive lynchets therefore dates to the 14th century or earlier. Within the Nature Reserve at Ravenhills Wood, Alfrick, and at Halesend Wood, Cradley, for instance, there is ridge-and-furrow (Hoverd 2003; Mindykowski and Bretherton 2003).

These and other examples represent agricultural or horticultural activity almost

Fig 3.13
Plan of the circular enclosure, a possible moat, and other features at Redmarley d'Abitot.

Fig 3.14
Strip lynchets near Clenchers Mill Lane represent medieval cultivation – agricultural or horticultural – on fairly steep slopes. This area, unlike some others cultivated in the medieval period, has not been allowed to revert to woodland.

certainly of medieval date, and indicate the extent to which the boundary between woodland and cultivated land has shifted back and forth. The chronology of this is uncertain, but the number of areas of ridge-and-furrow and lynchets suggest an episode of woodland shrinkage and increased arable production, possibly only for a short time. One possibility to account for this is that population pressure was such that food was in short supply, so that more marginal areas had to be put under the plough. Another possibility is that climatic deterioration made ploughing of the lower lying clay and silt areas increasingly difficult. Both factors might have come into play in the early 14th century, precisely the time the meagre dating evidence suggests (Hoverd 2003, 6, 38).

More specialised farming practices are also represented. At Coneygore Coppice, Alfrick, woodland survey found a number of features that defined the 'coney' (rabbit) warren – an oval enclosure formed by stone-revetted banks and ditches, containing two 'pillow mounds' (artificial warrens) (ibid). A pillow mound occupies a prominent position on Hollybush

Fig 3.15
Ridge-and-furrow around Birts Street and Rye Street, recorded from aerial photographs. The form of some of the ridges is typically medieval and the 'street' and 'green' place names suggest colonisation of a formerly wooded area fairly late in the medieval period. (Based on an Ordnance Survey map. © Crown copyright. All rights reserved. English Heritage licence no. 100019088.)

Hill, within the hillfort (Fig 3.16), and there is another just to the south of British Camp. These rabbit farms, if they are indeed of medieval date and not later, were the work of the lords of the manors.

At Donnington the steep south-facing slope of Haffield Bank, just to the west of the hillfort, has been partitioned with banks and terraces. This has been interpreted as a vineyard (RCHME 1932, 69-70). If this is so, then it is an outlier to the extensive medieval wine-producing area of the Vale of Gloucester (Finberg 1975, 66–7). Traces of the banks are still visible. The bishops of Hereford had other vineyards, now lost, at Cradley and Whitbourne (Hillaby 1997, 67–8).

The brackish expanses of Longdon Marsh and its neighbours had economic significance. Bond has suggested that they provided summer grazing when higher pastures might be parched (1981, 97), an idea perhaps reinforced by the drove way that runs along the northern margin of the Marsh (but outside the present study area). No doubt the marshes also provided waterfowl in abundance, a great asset to the Chase.

Quarries demonstrate another aspect of the working landscape. They are almost impossible to date unless found in direct relationships with other landscape features, but sometimes the form and arrangement of quarries – smaller, less organised and less intensive – suggests a medieval date. An example of this was found at Coneygore Coppice (Minykowski and Bretherton 2003). Another group of quarries that may be largely of medieval date – and that may indeed have much earlier origins – are those at Coombe Green (Fig 3.17; *and see* Fig 3.15). It is inherently likely that some of the many quarries on and around the hills are of medieval date, for the churches of the area are largely built of local stone.

Woodland industries themselves have left their mark on the landscape. Deep V-shaped gullies, narrower than normal hollow-ways, have developed where felled timber has been hauled out of the woods, as at Ravenshill. Whether any of these are of medieval date is uncertain, but their relationship to woodland boundaries with venerable coppiced small-leaved limes suggests considerable antiquity (ibid, 10). Numerous charcoal pitsteads have been noted in woodlands across the area but these are undated (eg Grubb and Derham 2003, 10, 24, 26; Hoverd 2003, passim).

Other work of an 'industrial' nature at this period is not immediately apparent in the landscape. Decorative floor tiles were being

Fig 3.16
Pillow mound on Hollybush Hill. The walkers' shelter on the summit of Midsummer Hill can be seen to the left, beyond the deep wooded ravine. The mound itself was believed to be a Neolithic long barrow in the 19th century and was excavated on that assumption. The archaeologist General Augustus Pitt Rivers persuaded the local antiquarians of its true nature – an artificial rabbit warren of medieval or early post-medieval date (Hilton Price 1887, 218–20).

made at Great Malvern Priory in the 15th century and two of the kilns have been found. The products were widely distributed across the West Midlands, and reached as far as Dorset, Pembroke, Sussex and Derbyshire (B Smith1978, 71). However, the traditional Malvern pottery industry (*see* Chapter 2) had migrated eastwards to Hanley Castle.

The religious landscape

It is impossible to divide religious aspects of medieval life from secular. However, although the bishops and abbots may appear to have been to some extent politically motivated, there were people who had genuine religious belief, people for whom the churches and the holy wells had real meaning. It has been suggested that in prehistory several areas (the environs of Stonehenge and Avebury, famously, for example, but perhaps also the Malverns in a more subtle way) can be seen as 'ritual landscapes'. It is tempting to consider the Malvern Hills as a 'ritual landscape' in the medieval period as much as in the prehistoric periods.

There are significant churches – the minster at Ledbury and St Mary's, Dymock, which might have been the centre of a Christian community since the time of the Celtic Church if Leech (1981, 31) is right. With the break-up of the minsters' *parochia*, probably in the 12th century, new parish churches were established to either side of the Hills. To the Hills themselves had come the hermits and holy men, and their deliberate successors, the Benedictines at Great and Little Malvern. The Hills are a 'desert', inhabited by ancient practices and spirits, and the priories are not ordinary parish churches, but rather the bases of religious 'elite forces'. There are other intriguing hints of the existence of small chapels or shrines on the Hills. On the summit of Midsummer Hill are the footings of a small single-celled rectangular building oriented east-west and with an entrance (probably) in the western end (*see* Fig 2.13, **c**). Was this a shrine? However, the holy wells perhaps, rather than any other building, are what make the Malverns special in this respect (Fig 3.18).

One version of the founding legend of Great Malvern declares that the priory was founded in 1085 by two monks, Aldwin and Guy, after a

Fig 3.17
Grassed-over quarries on Coombe Green Common. These are probably medieval and possibly even earlier in origin. The cultivation remains visible at top left are probably also of medieval date.

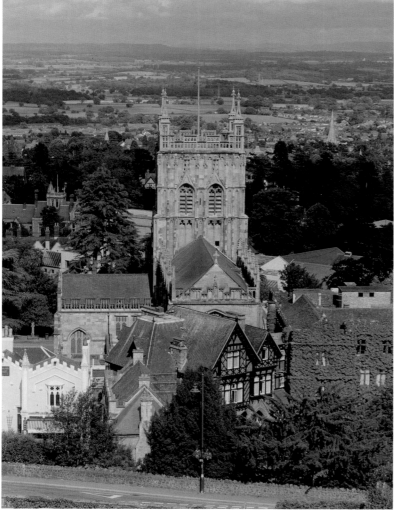

struggle in the Malvern wilderness that lasted for many years. Although they despaired, declaring that it would be better to die on pilgrimage to Jerusalem than to remain any longer at Malvern, they were persuaded to persevere. In another version the priory owed its existence to St Werstan, who in the time of Edward the Confessor, was shown by angels a small cave for a hermitage at Malvern. Werstan was martyred but a chapel of St Michael was later raised on the site of his hermitage near St Ann's Well (B Smith 1978, 41–3). That Werstan's story maintained its importance to the monks (unless, indeed, they invented it) is shown by its incorporation in the church windows installed in the 15th century.

Regardless of the truth of these tales it is certain that Great Malvern was a daughter house of Westminster. Nevertheless, the Priory maintained close relations with the bishops and priors of Worcester, who attempted to wrest control of Great Malvern from Westminster. The dispute came to a head in the late 13th century and involved not only the Archbishop of Canterbury, but also the King. The story is given in detail by Brian Smith (ibid, 46–53) but the end result was that Westminster retained its control, although in practice the priors of Great Malvern retained a degree of independence. The details of the foundation of Little Malvern Priory are at least as confused as those of Great Malvern, but there is no doubt that it was always dependent on Worcester (ibid, 93–5).

The Priory church at Great Malvern (Fig 3.19) lies directly below St Ann's Well – implicated in its foundation myth – and close to another spring, Hay Well. At Little Malvern (Fig 3.20) there also seems to be a link with natural water sources, notably Ditchford's Well (now lost) and the springs now under the British Camp Reservoir. It is well known that great efforts were made to supply monasteries with water, but this is nearly always explained in purely practical terms. The water is needed either to drink or to cleanse (eg Aston1993, 20). Like many such functionalist explanations this falls down on the question of why other large medieval communal institutions of status – such as castles, great houses, palaces – did not apparently require such elaborate water supplies. The answer must be that the relationship between monasteries and water has a religious, as well as a practical, aspect. For the monks, physical cleanliness was an affirmation of spiritual cleanliness (Greene 1992, 116–17).

Other Malvern springs that seem to have had a religious connotation in the medieval period include the Holy Well, St Thomas's Well (Mathon) and St Catherine's Well (Leigh).

Much ink has been spilt on the topic of the exact location of Piers Plowman's dream in William Langland's poem, written in the 1360s. Most recent authorities have decided in favour of Pewtress Well, on the west side of the hills immediately to the north of Herefordshire Beacon (B Smith 1978, 89). However, the site of the dream is an idealised romantic landscape subverted for Langland's religious and political ends, and in any case the description is borrowed directly from an earlier French ballad, so even if it was a real landscape it would be a French one (Robert Hook pers comm). The 'broad bank by the side of a stream' where Piers lay down was a generic rather than a specific place that can be identified in the landscape. Nevertheless, the fitness of this idealised landscape with the real Malvern landscape of his youth can not have been lost on Langland.

Post-medieval and later (1540–present)

Transition from a 'medieval' to a 'post-medieval' way of life came late and gradually in the Malverns. The suppression of the two priories had a profound effect, but at Little Malvern even this was mitigated by the retention of the manor in the hands of a catholic recusant family. Little Malvern remained a catholic community (B Smith 1978, 120–1). Hanley also retained a strong catholic minority (Hurle 1978, 50–1, 57). At Great Malvern the passing of the priory was a matter for regret, for it had been perceived as having a real usefulness to the community (B Smith 1978, 107).

Main agents of change were the disafforestation of the Chase (Hurle 1978, 43–5;

Fig 3.18 (opposite, top) St Ann's Well, a spring of religious significance in the medieval period. The pump room and octagon were constructed during the 19th century.

Fig 3.19 (opposite, bottom) Great Malvern Priory Church seen from above to the west, on the path to St Ann's Well.

Fig 3.20 (above) Little Malvern Priory occupies a similar topographical niche to its sister priory.

Fig 3.21
Plan of the
enclosure on
Hangman's Hill.

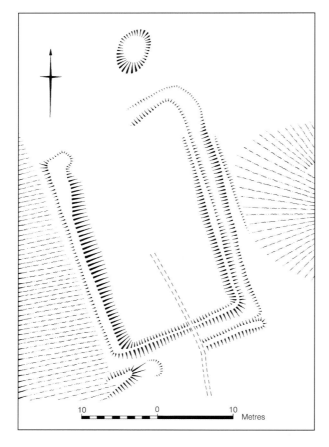

10   0   10
Metres

Weaver 1998) and the draining of the marshes (Bond 1981, 104–10), neither of which occurred until well into the 17th century or later. Disafforestation came with the decision by Charles I to sell the Chase in about 1630. This led to rioting among those who believed they were about to lose their common rights (Weaver 1998, 210). The pattern of dispersed farmsteads continued, or was perhaps even enhanced as a result of disafforestation and enclosure. Encroachments onto the remaining commons were made in vast numbers, reaching epidemic proportions in the 19th century (ibid, 214). The results are still clearly to be seen, around Huntsbridge for instance, as they are on Bringsty Common to the north-west of the Hills. Even Malvern itself, despite its growing spa status, remained a small village until the middle of the 19th century.

Disafforestation ended centuries of restrictions on agriculture and enabled 17th- and 18th-century landowners to go ahead with improvements. The arable and meadows of Baldenhall (Barnard's Green and Hall Green) had been enclosed as early as 1550, although they were still thrown open to common grazing after harvest (B Smith 1978, 142).

Enclosure led to rioting at Leigh in 1776 and murder at Berrow in 1780 (Weaver 1998, 211–12). However, it was not until 1797 that Hanley's commons were enclosed. Enclosure also facilitated the development of new farming practices. In a tributary valley to the River Leadon near Dymock, now occupied by the M50 motorway, there are the fragmentary remains of a floated water meadow. The origin of controlled flooding of water meadows, to bring on an early grass crop and generally to improve the grazing, is now thought to be earlier than was previously believed, but this example is likely to be of the 17th or 18th century. Stock farming continued to be as important as it no doubt had been in earlier periods, although a change in emphasis from cattle to sheep is noted about 1600 (B Smith 1978, 141). An earthwork site that may be relevant is a rectangular embanked enclosure, with no visible internal features, occupying a slight saddle on Hangman's Hill (Fig 3.21; *and see* Fig 3.6). Although the date and function of this feature are by no means certain, perhaps the most likely explanation is that it is the remains of a pound for stock grazing the Hills. The relative crispness of the slight earthworks suggests a recent date, although this is by no means decisive. Boundary earthworks of similar form are also to be seen on the Hills in this area.

Fig 3.22
Damson orchards were
once a characteristic
feature of the area, but are
now a rarity.

Orchards, particularly of apple, pear and damson, were a feature of the landscape and of the economy of the area that is now much diminished (Fig 3.22). However, the trace of former orchards is still to be seen in the relatively regular, straight blocks of ridge-and-furrow orchard planting. This is a particularly distinctive feature on aerial photographs of the region.

Later, more systematic enclosure had an effect not only on the agricultural regime, but also, perhaps, even more significantly for the present landscape, on the road system (Hurle 1978, 134–5). The regular enclosures and their straight roads have given a north–south and east–west regularity to the landscape between the Hills and the River Severn, quite alien to its previous state. However, fragments of the older landscape can be seen, not only on the surviving commons, but in features such as the footpath that sweeps from north-west to south-east to the south of Blackmore Park Farm. This appears as a road on Taylor's 1722 map of Worcestershire (ibid, 132) and its position and shape suggest that it may also follow part of the medieval pale of Blackmore Park. However, although the path follows a substantial hedge bank with pollarded trees, there is no other sign of a pale.

Agriculture was the dominant economic activity of the area, but other trades were also pursued. The traditional woodland industries continued, although in gradual decline. Many of the woodland features previously mentioned, such as woodland banks, logging tracks and charcoal burning pitsteads, were still in use. The distribution of charcoal-burning pitsteads may be significant. While many are isolated, suggesting small-scale activity, there are a number of larger clusters, indicating larger-scale production, possibly over a long period (Hoverd 2003, 39). What industry or industries this charcoal production was supplying is not known, but the potters of Hanley Castle might have been principal customers. Charcoal burning implies coppice wood management and much coppiced woodland can still be seen around the Hills (Fig 3.23).

Many weavers are recorded (B Smith 1978, 143–4). Tanning and gloving were also important and have left their mark in numerous place names (Goodbury 1999, passim). The significance of quarrying and related trades, up to the 20th century, is all too obvious in the landscape. One rather neglected aspect of this is lime burning, which has left the remains of some sixteen limekilns in the parishes of Colwall, Cradley, Ledbury and Mathon (Goodbury 1999, appendix). More limekilns might have been expected, but recent large-scale quarrying might have destroyed some, while many

limekilns were temporary structures designed to consume themselves (Hoverd 2003, 34–5). Less successful attempts at mineral extraction were the coal mine (*see* Chapter 1) and a gold mine to the north of The Wyche, which had started by the late 16th century and was not abandoned until more than 100 years later (B Smith 1978, 173–4). There is too much later quarrying in this area for any recognisable remains of the gold mine to survive above ground.

Of greater significance in the landscape than any industry, however, has been the growth of the spa at Malvern. From this developed, especially on the northern hills, a landscape of leisure – of paths and carriage drives, benches and shelters, ornamental buildings – as well as the distinctive townscape of Great Malvern itself (Fig 3.24). At the same time there is a development of polite landscapes around the major houses, especially Eastnor Castle. The extensive park here was laid out in the early 19th century. An interesting feature here is Clutter's

Fig 3.23
A grown-out coppice stool; this one is near Walm's Well but the woods around the Hills are rich in evidence of coppice management.

Fig 3.24
Great Malvern. The expansive spread of this early Victorian spa town is brilliantly illustrated in a series of low-level oblique aerial photographs, taken by Harold Wingham in November 1951.

Fig 3.25
Clutter's Cave. Although it is probably a relatively recent creation – part of the 'polite' landscape of Eastnor Park – Clutter's Cave is a particularly apposite feature, given the probable status of the Hills in the early medieval period as a spiritual battleground for hermits and holy men.

Cave (Fig 3.25), which has been popularly thought of as a medieval hermit's refuge and has attracted numerous legends (B Smith 1978, 9). However, it does not seem to have been recorded before the mid-19th century and it is probably a grotto belonging to Eastnor Park. It may be significant that its entrance faces directly towards the obelisk erected in 1812 to commemorate various members of the Somers and Cocks families (*see* Fig 1.2).

Continuing encroachment on the commons throughout the 19th century led to the Malvern Hills Act of 1884 and the creation of the Malvern Hills Conservators, whose powers were extended by further Acts in the 20th century. The Hills were designated an Area of Outstanding Natural Beauty (AONB) in 1959 (B Smith 1978, 247–8).

Changes to the landscape in the 20th century are too numerous and too well known to describe in detail here. However, the traces of the Second World War are worth mentioning. Camps, searchlight batteries (of which traces of seven have been recorded), pillboxes, the military hospitals around Great Malvern, and the Prisoner of War camps in Eastnor Park and Blackmore Park have all left their mark, in the shape of earthworks or surviving structures. Several of these have found adaptive uses in the present. The trackways of the Eastnor Prisoner of War camp now serve a caravan site. Another – much slighter – recent feature, probably of military origin, was found at the extreme northern end of British Camp (*see* Fig 2.12 **k**). Here a crescentic earthwork overlies and cuts into the hillfort counterscarp bank. Immediately above it on the rampart is a slight rectangular depression with a low mound behind, preventing it from being seen on the skyline when viewed from below. These are probably a gun emplacement and a slit trench, positioned so as to enfilade the road climbing up to Wynds Point from the east.

4
Overview

The Malvern Hills can be seen for miles and provide a dramatic contrast to the surrounding low ground, particularly of the Severn Valley. The symbolic importance of such natural places, particularly of dramatic hills on the one hand and of springs on the other, as providing interfaces with the spirit worlds, is widely known from ethnographical research (eg Hirsch and O'Hanlon 1995), and their role within social and ritual landscapes is now discussed extensively within archaeology (eg Ashmore and Knapp 1999; Bradley 2000). It is important to ask how the hills would have been viewed from the early settlements in the surrounding lowlands. Were they imbued with legend or invested with origin myths? The springs make the Malvern Hills special in this respect, and this is an interesting and important theme throughout the human occupation of the area, from prehistory to the present (Figs 4.1, 4.4 and 4.5). The drama of the hills themselves has been enhanced both by their spiritual associations and by their traditional use for grazing while much of the surrounding area has been well wooded and settled.

The apparent longevity of major boundaries supports the view that has become prevalent among archaeologists researching the English landscape, that boundaries are more stable than settlements. This too is an important theme in the history of the Malverns. The Malvern Hills have been a borderland, in one sense or another, probably since the Later Bronze Age, at least.

'Industry', in various forms, is another important thread running through the history of the Malverns. Pottery was being manufactured here from the mid Iron Age until the 17th century AD. This was not a continuous activity; there was a hiatus in the early medieval period, after which the industry shifted its focus eastwards to Hanley Castle. Quarrying and woodland industries also have a respectable antiquity here. These very long-lived industries are all certainly worthy of further study. The fluctuating demands on land, for agriculture on the one hand and for woodland products on the other, is reflected in the cultivation remains found within many 'ancient' woods. Despite being a woodland region it is clear that at some periods, especially in the high Middle Ages, arable agriculture expanded to a remarkable degree in response to rising population and falling yields.

How does contemporary society value the Hills? How should their distinctive character be conserved and the components that make up this character preserved? Successful conservation and management can only come from an understanding of the deep-rooted significance of the Hills as a cultural landscape.

Future research

Themes

Some themes for research can be identified. In the earliest periods attention should be directed to the sand and gravel terraces – well suited to prehistoric occupation – around Mathon and Cradley. This is where the single Palaeolithic artefact of the area was found. Fieldwalking of areas where the ploughsoil has yielded artefacts of the earliest periods should have some priority. It is remarkable that in an area with an important Iron Age and Roman ceramic industry not one pottery kiln structure has been identified. Geophysical survey of the known areas of production followed by targeted excavation may yield important results.

The 'missing' early medieval period is a research gap of high priority, but it is one that is difficult to address through a conventional research programme because we do not yet know what we are looking for; discoveries are more likely to come about serendipitously. However, if the characterisation of the Hills at this period as a 'wilderness' – in the sense perhaps intended by William of Malmesbury – is correct, then any search for conventional archaeological 'sites' may be misplaced. In the medieval period further research into the development of the settlement pattern would refine understanding. This would involve study of the moated sites, further study and survey of earthworks and the study of standing buildings – an aspect that this project did not address. Such work, in particular, would make a thoroughly worthwhile research project for a local group of independent archaeologists and historians. What status did the motte-and-bailey sites represent? Are they obviously 'castles' or are they more akin to the fancy moats, which later became part of the range of distinctive settlement types of the area?

These suggestions will be put in a regional context by the publication of the West Midlands Archaeological Research Framework (Watt forthcoming).

The current project has, it is hoped, changed the emphasis by seeing the Malvern Hills and their surroundings as a distinctive landscape – a spiritual battleground and boundary zone, and an area for special ritualised secular activity, such as hunting. Research of a type that has taken place at Glastonbury (Rahtz and Watts 2003), another 'special' place with a Benedictine monastery, may identify possible directions for future study.

Approaches

Most of the new discoveries from aerial photography noted here were only made because of the aerial reconnaissance done as part of this project. These sites are not visible on earlier photography and this fact emphasises just how successful this programme of flying was, and how important it will be to undertake further aerial photography of this area in the future. There are undoubtedly more sites waiting to be discovered.

More importantly, however, there is a definite bias to the distribution of cropmark evidence. There is a distinct 'cropmark zone', reflected in the distributions of ring ditches and later prehistoric enclosures,

for example, around the southern fringes of the Hills just below the 200m contour. It is also noteworthy that nothing of the major Roman settlement at Dymock shows on available aerial photography. This, as in most of the project area, is probably due to the prevalence of pasture and a lack of previous reconnaissance, combined with unpropitious conditions for aerial reconnaissance over grass during the period of the project. Much evidence for earlier periods may be hidden under pasture, medieval and later cultivation, and beneath current settlement. This possibility needs to be tested.

The great success of the woodland element of the project suggests that more work in the wooded areas would be fruitful. This work should be targeted both to further reconnaissance – to identify new sites and landscape features – and to more

Fig 4.1
The Earl Beauchamp Fountain, Cowleigh Road. The legend reads: 'This fountain was presented to the people of Cowleigh by William, Earl Beauchamp, 1905'. The fountain has been restored recently by the AONB and a consortium of other bodies.

detailed analytical survey to develop understanding of particular areas. The possible prehistoric features in Frith Wood and the extensive cultivation remains under woodland on Crews Hill stand out as clear candidates for further research. More detailed work on the archaeology of Ravenshill Wood could yield particular benefits in terms of public access and education through the Nature Reserve. A surprising amount of the area covered by the survey is under arable cultivation. Systematic fieldwalking to recover or map the distribution of artefacts in ploughed fields would be very productive, especially for early – and particularly the earliest – periods.

Excavation is an intrusive and to some extent destructive archaeological technique and, like marriage, should not be entered into unadvisedly, lightly or wantonly. There is a tension between conservation and research in this respect. Nevertheless, in order to resolve the chronological questions that are so fundamental to our understanding of human habitation and activity, targeted excavation is absolutely necessary. Archaeology is nothing if it is not a research discipline, and if we are to be properly inquisitive about the past some excavation must take place. In an area that has seen, comparatively, so little excavation in the past, this becomes a priority. The ring ditches, field systems and enclosures found by aerial photography provide very little information unless their date is known. At present, with the exception of the site at Cradley, these sites are floating within a chronological void that covers not just centuries but millennia. The dates of even the most prominent prehistoric monuments, the hillforts, are unknown in detail. The two radiocarbon dates from Midsummer Hill, while better than nothing, are a drop in the ocean of our lack of knowledge. Developer-funded excavation is unlikely, one would hope, to be a major factor within an AONB. The development of properly formulated research excavations, therefore, must be promoted and embraced.

Another crucial area of knowledge that can only be resolved by excavation – even if only on a very small scale – is that of past environments. Environmental archaeology has barely been touched upon here, because the evidence is almost entirely lacking. The ebb and flow of woodland can be traced for the later historical period from the trees and plants living in the landscape now, but for earlier periods the canvas is blank and the state of plant and animal populations can only be inferred from indirect evidence. Sampling for pollen and other plant fossils, insect remains and animal bones, and other environmental indicators from sequences of dated deposits alone can resolve these questions.

Archaeology is about the excitement of discovery but it is also, at least as much, about the excitement of analysis and understanding. The very basic questions asked here are a means to an end – a continually refined understanding of human society and activity on and around this iconic range of hills. Archaeology must go forward as a discipline because only then can interest be sustained. If future generations are to be enthused about the ancient landscape and to continue to care for it, the story must be carried forward by answers to these questions and, more importantly, the formulation of new and better questions.

Conservation: trees, rabbits and people

The name Malvern – 'Bald Hill' – implies that the Hills were substantially cleared at an early date and grazing animals have maintained open grassland on the ridge probably fairly continuously over the centuries. However, the decline in grazing since the Second World War has led to the regeneration of scrub on the flanks of the hills and succession to larger tree growth. Aerial photographs taken up to the late 1950s show the area around British Camp, for instance, free of trees (Fig 4.2). By 1979 young trees were beginning to colonise the ditch and counterscarp near the north-eastern edge of the fort and scrub was encroaching on the south-western ramparts (eg NMR: SO 7640/7). By the 1990s, large parts of the ramparts at the northern and southern ends of the fort had been overtaken by scrub and some large trees (Figs 4.3). A programme of clearance has now been undertaken, with a long term scheme to re-introduce grazing animals to the hills. Although this will maintain the traditional landscape, the traditional lifestyle that gave rise to

Fig 4.2
British Camp in 1958 –
still a 'bald hill'. (Aerial
photograph by Harold
Wingham.)

Fig 4.3
British Camp in 1999.
Scrub is encroaching on
the flanks of the hill and
has reached the ramparts
in places; succession to
larger trees is taking place.

it is hardly capable of resurrection. Nevertheless, even in the short term, the removal of scrub and colonising trees from the ancient earthworks of British Camp is greatly to be welcomed.

Bracken is also invading the hills. At Midsummer Hill, where it covers a substantial part of the interior of the hillfort, this is likely to be a serious issue. Measures to combat this problem are already in hand, but the use of heavy machinery itself, in schemes such as this, needs to be monitored carefully.

The greatest immediate danger to the earthworks on the Hills is from burrowing animals. Rabbits in epidemic numbers are doing untold damage at British Camp and Midsummer Hill. In view of the medieval or early post-medieval efforts to breed rabbits at both sites this is somewhat ironic. Visitor erosion, from walkers, mountain bikers and, at Midsummer Hill, horse riders, is also an issue.

Beyond the Hills, the normal everyday operations of agriculture, forestry, other industries and development are the agents of changes that affect the historic landscape.

Management action and monitoring

The management action and monitoring phase of the current project will seek to address these issues. Following closely on the survey reported here, this programme will attempt to secure improved care for both known and newly discovered sites and historic landscape features. This work may involve the delineation of fragile landscapes and the development of policies for their protection, designation of particular sites for further protection at a national or local level, and continued monitoring of conditions at selected locations. Local landowners and managers will be invited to participate, either through Countryside Stewardship schemes – under which archaeological sites falling within such schemes will be noted as in receipt of specific protective measures – or through discussions to secure formal or informal agreements concerning the care of sites and monuments.

The results of these schemes should include:

- formal management plans for a limited number of particularly vulnerable sites,

- integration of an archaeological element into the management plans of all landholdings,

- enhanced protection for significant sites, promotion of information on grants, Countryside Stewardship and similar schemes,

- and new guidance and improved information on individual areas of the landscape, linked to policies and local designations.

The information arising from this exercise can also be tailored for wider public dissemination and can inform the sustainable tourism strategy for the Malvern Hills AONB. Specific areas of the countryside not previously well known or historically understood can be promoted through self-guided trails, for example, to relieve pressure on the 'honeypot' localities. This is already being achieved through the publication of 'Discovery Walk' leaflets.

Together, the two phases of the project – survey and management – will combine to secure a more reliable record and fuller understanding of the historic landscape, and benchmarks for its sustainable management. The key to success lies in partnerships between diverse organisations and individuals, and integration of the needs of the natural and the cultural environment.

Buildings and earthworks created with infinite care and labour, and historic landscape features that have developed organically can survive for hundreds or even thousands of years. They are fragile, however, and in the face of powerful modern machinery, can be destroyed in minutes. The task facing us is to manage legitimate development and change, so as to minimise the damage to the historic environment and to eliminate unnecessary destruction. In this way we hope that the distinctive character and magic of the Hills (Figs 4.4 and 4.5) can best be preserved for future generations.

Fig 4.4
St Ann's Well, interior.

Fig 4.5
'Malvhina', the latest
apotheosis of the Malvern
water spirit.

Appendix 1
Gazetteer of prehistoric, Roman and medieval sites

Many of the sites of archaeological interest mentioned in this book are on private land and may only be visited with the owners' permission. Sites marked with asterisks have visible remains and are open to public access or can be seen from Public Rights of Way.

Sites are given with their National Grid Reference and National Monuments Record number or, where more appropriate, their county Sites and Monuments Record number. In a few cases a published reference is given instead.

For reasons of space, the gazetteer omits some relatively common classes of site or landscape feature: findspots, lynchets, ridge-and-furrow, boundaries, quarries and tracks. A fine set of strip lynchets can be seen at the southern end of Frith Wood, Ledbury (SO 714 389). Good examples of ridge-and-furrow are found near Brook Farm, Leigh Sinton (SO 787 506), between Smith End Green and Leigh (at SO 777 528) and on the steep east-facing slopes to the south of Coombe Green Common (SO 778 362). In winter, ridge-and-furrow can be seen beneath the trees within the Nature Reserve at Ravenshill Wood (SO 738 534). The early quarries on Coombe Green Common (SO 776 365) are among the best preserved and most interesting in the area. The path between the south-eastern corner of Malvern Common (SO 789 438) and Lower Arles Wood (SO 800 431) follows a fine hedgebank with pollarded trees. Good examples of coppice stools can be seen in Frith Wood, Ledbury, near Walm's Well and near Cale's Farm. An excellent series of hollow-ways descends the eastern flank of Swinyard Hill to the south of Foxhall (SO 764 382) and there are also some good pollards near the road across Berrow Downs here.

Barrows, ring ditches, and related prehistoric earthworks

Bradlow Knoll* (SO 716 390; SO 73 NW 130)
Donnington (SO 720 333; SO 73 SW 38 & 39)
Dymock (SO 726 330; SO 73 SW 33)
Dymock (SO 722 332; SO 73 SW 73)
New Mills, Ledbury (SO 700 386; SO 73 NW 100)
Pinnacle Hill* (SO 768 421; SO 74 SE 6)
Redmarley d'Abitot (SO 742 314; SO 73 SW 32)
Redmarley d'Abitot (SO 757 338; SO 73 SE 53)
South End, Mathon (SO 737 448; SO 74 SW 1)
Worcestershire Beacon (SO 768 452; SO 74 NE 16)

Prehistoric field systems

Donnington (SO 727 328; SO 73 SW 40)
Donnington (SO 721 327: SO 73 SW 42)
Frith Wood, Ledbury (SO 714 392; (Hoverd 2000a, 48))

Prehistoric settlements

Brockamin, Leigh (SO 766 533; W07030)
Cotheridge (SO 788 539; SO 75 SE 52)
Cradley (SO 714 479; SO 74 NW 39)
Cradley (SO 752 492; SO 74 NE 67)
Donnington (SO 720 333; SO 73 SW 37)
Donnington (SO 727 329; SO 73 SW 41)
Donnington (SO 721 328; SO 73 SW 43)
Donnington (SO 703 337; SO 73 SW 45 & 46)
Frith Wood, Ledbury* (SO 714 392; (Hoverd 2000a, 48))
Pendock (SO 789 326; SO 73 SE 44)
Playley Green (SO 76 31; SO 73 SE 18)
Russell's End (SO 744 330; SO 73 SW 31)

Hillforts

Berrow Hill (SO 745 585; SO 75 NW 3)
British Camp★ (SO 760 400; SO 74 SE 3)
Gadbury Bank (SO 79 31; SO 73 SE 1)
Haffield Camp (SO 72 33; SO 73 SW 10)
Midsummer Hill★ (SO 760 375; SO 73 NE 11)

Roman kiln sites

Buckman's Farm (East) (SO 788 496; W01315)
Crumpton Hill (East) (SO 760 480; H10649)
Donnington (SO 70 33; H3713)
Dysons Perrins School (SO 775 483; W25262)
Eastwood Road (SO 779 485; W27243)
Grit Farm (East) (SO 778 490; W04585)
Grit Farm (North) (SO 777 494; W11392)
Half Key Lane (SO 772 487; W07061)
Holder Station (SO 786 491; W27051)
Hygienic Laundry (SO 778 481; W06004)
Leigh (SO 792 499; W26398)
Lower Howsell (SO 785 485; W23935 & 27882)
Malvern (SO 782 499; W03700)
Newland Common (SO 791 486; W01510)
Newland Hopfield (SO 792 480; W04072)
Oakfields Farm (SO 775 493; W27117)
Swan Inn (SO 793 489; W04073)
Townsend Farm (SO 790 482; W09317)
Upper Sandlin Farm, Leigh (tile) (SO 758 512; SO 75 SE 1)

Roman settlement and other industrial sites

Berrow Farm, Martley (SO 744 586; W30834)
Chase High School/DERA (SO 787 447; W30058, etc)
Cotheridge (SO 782 545; W25812)
Cowleigh Park Farm (SO 766 475; W25986)
Donnington (SO 700 330; SO 73 SW 12)
Dymock (SO 70 31; SO 73 SW 1 & 25)
Lower Howsell (SO 785 485; W23935 & 27882)
Malvern Link (SO 791 481; W27017)
North End Farm, Madresfield (SO 79 48; SO 74 NE 58)
Oyster Hill (SO 722 417; SO 74 SW 111)
Worcester Road, Malvern (SO 788 480; W27049)

Priories

Great Malvern★ (SO 776 458; SO 74 NE 6 & 50)
Little Malvern★ (SO 770 404; SO 74 SE 1 & 33)

Churches

Alfrick★ (SO 748 529; SO 75 SW 22)
Berrow★ (SO 793 343; SO 73 SE 15)
Bransford★ (SO 797 515; SO 75 SE 29)
Bromsberrow★ (SO 742 336; SO 73 SW 77)
Castlemorton★ (SO 795 372; SO 73 NE 24)
Coddington★ (SO 718 426; SO 74 SW 38)
Colwall★ (SO 739 423; SO 74 SW 44)
Cotheridge★ (SO 786 547; SO 75 SE 23)
Cradley★ (SO 736 471; SO 74 NW 36)
Donnington★ (SO 708 342; SO 73 SW 21)
Dymock★ (SO 700 312; SO 73 SW 14)
Eastnor★ (SO 731 372; SO 73 NW 62)
Ledbury★ (SO 715 377; SO 73 NW 55)
Leigh★ (SO 784 534; SO 75 SE 22)
Mathon★ (SO 733 458; SO 74 NW 35)
Newland (SO 797 484; SO 74 NE 12)
Redmarley d'Abitot (SO 752 313; SO 73 SE 73)
Suckley★ (SO 721 516; SO 75 SW 93)
Whitbourne★ (SO 725 569; SO 75 NW 50)

Castles

Castle Green, Leigh★ (SO 780 519; SO 75 SE 4)
Castlemorton★ (SO 794 371; SO 73 NE 4)
Herefordshire Beacon★ (SO 760 400; SO 74 SE 3)

Medieval settlement

This section includes a variety of evidence, including standing buildings, field remains and cropmarks, and a variety of settlement types from town to single dwelling.

Abbot's Lodge, Ledbury (SO 711 377; SO 73 NW 30)
Alfrick (SO 745 531; SO 75 SW 74)
Ankerdine Farm, Doddenham (SO 731 565; SO 75 NW 71)
Barnards, Eldersfield (SO 795 309; SO 73 SE 28)
Berrow (SO 794 343; SO 73 SE 7)
Birts Street (SO 788 363; SO 73 NE 30)
Bradburn's Farm, Whitbourne (SO 723 571; SO 75 NW 24)

Bransford (SO 798 515; SO 75 SE 13)
Burton's Farm, Wellington Heath (SO 701 401; SO 74 SW 28)
Bury Court, Redmarley d'Abitot (SO 760 328; SO 73 SE 3)
Castlemorton* (SO 792 373; SO 73 NE 16 & 25)
Coddington (SO 722 424; SO 74 SW 101)
Colwall* (SO 738 423; SO 74 SW 37)
Coombegreen Common (SO 778 362; SO 73 NE 31)
Cotheridge (SO 786 543; SO 75 SE 14)
Cradley* (SO 736 471; SO 74 NW 1)
Doddenham (SO 737 579; SO 75 NW 10)
Donnington* (SO 707 349; SO 73 SW 44)
Downhouse, Redmarley d'Abitot (SO 771 302; SO 73 SE 24)
Dymock* (SO 700 312; SO 73 SW 23)
Eastnor (SO 736 372; SO 73 NW 89)
Epiphany Bridge, Leigh (SO 749 517; SO 75 SW 92)
Fincher's Farm, Whitbourne (SO 721 573; SO 75 NW 26)
Fowlet Farm, Eastnor (SOP 752 363; SO 73 NE 42)
Gamage Hall, Dymock (SO 709 305; SO 73 SW 3 & 60)
Graftons Farm, Birtsmorton (SO 777 369; SO 73 NE 62)
Hayes Coppice, Berrow (SO 754 348; SO 73 SE 50)
Hollybush* (SO 765 365; SO 73 NE 50)
Howler's Coppice, Eastnor (SO 7436 3597; SO 73 NW 78)
Knightwick (SO 728 552; SO 75 NW 7)
Ledbury* (SO 710 376; SO 73 NW 19)
Note: Individual medieval buildings within Ledbury are also listed separately in the NMR.
Little Woolpits, Ledbury (SO 723 354; SO 73 NW 111)
Lower House Farm, Leigh Sinton (SO 778 512; SO 75 SE 65)
Lower Poswick, Whitbourne (SO 708 571; SO 75 NW 40)
Lower Tedney, Whitbourne (SO 727 589; SO 75 NW 48)
Lower Whiting Farm, Berrow (SO 787 347; SO 73 SE 63)
Malvern (SO 788 468; SO 74 NE 33 & 53)
Massington (SO 740 395; SO 73 NW 8)
Ockeridge Farm, Ledbury (SO 751 398; SO 73 NE 83)
Old Colwall (SO 731 418; SO 74 SW 67)
Old Ground Coppice, Castlemorton (SO 766 369; SO 73 NE 56)
Peg's Farm, Wellington Heath (SO 702 411; SO 74 SW 10)

Pendock* (SO 790 327; SO 73 SE 32 & 45)
Ravenhills Wood, Alfrick* (SO 735 537; SO 75 SW 91)
Russell's End (SO 747 331; SO 73 SW 78)
South Hyde Farm, Mathon (SO 737 440; SO 74 SW 76)
Suckley (SO 721 516; SO 75 SW 9)
Suckley Manor (SO 708 510; SO 75 SW 7)
Tinker's Grove, Eastnor (SO 7441 3735; SO 73 NW 85)
Upper Hall, Ledbury (SO 713 378; SO 73 NW 29)
Upper House Farm, Eastnor (SO 754 368; SO 73 NE 44)
Wayend Street, Eastnor (SO 740 365; SO 73 NW 76 & 77)
Whitbourne (SO 724 569; SO 75 NW 21)
White House Farm, Eastnor (SO 728 385; SO 73 NW 53)

Moats

(This list includes some doubtful examples.)
Alfrick Court (SO 748 531; SO 75 SW 13)
Aubrey's Farm, Bromsberrow (SO 755 337; SO 73 SE 4)
Berrow (SO 767 351; SO 73 NE 2)
Berrow (SO 792 348; SO 73 SE 61)
Brockbury, Colwall (SO 745 418; SO 74 SW 7)
Bronsil Castle (SO 749 372; SO 73 NW 5)
Church Farm, Mathon (SO 732 457; SO 74 NW 5)
Cleeve House, Pendock (SO 797 330; SO 73 SE 2)
Court Farm, Berrow (SO 793 342; SO 73 SE 8)
Cowleigh Park Farm (SO 766 476; SO 74 NE 44)
Cummins Farm, Colwall (SO 738 409; SO 74 SW 3)
Donnington (SO 704 347; SO 73 SW 11)
Donnington* (SO 708 340; SO 73 SW 13)
Hilltop Farm, Eldersfield (SO 798 322; SO 73 SE 12)
Howsen, Cotheridge (SO 795 541; SO 75 SE 17)
Knight's Green, Dymock (SO 710 319; SO 73 SW 2)
Leigh Court (SO 783 534; SO 75 SE 19)
Leigh Sinton (SO 782 507; SO 75 SE 8)
Lulsley (SO 746 555; SO 75 NW 8)
Moat Court (Sherrard's Green), Malvern (SO 799 462; SO 74 NE 3)
Moat Farmhouse, Mathon (SO 745 447; SO 74 SW 2)
Moat Meadow, Eastnor* (SO 7204 3873; SO 73 NW 61)

Newland Grange (SO 794 496; SO 74 NE 40)

Oldcastle Farm, Colwall (SO 753 406; SO 74 SE 5)

Pipe Elm Farm, Leigh (SO 775 507; SO 75 SE 20)

Redmarley d'Abitot★ (SO 758 309; SO 73 SE 19)

Seed Farm, Cradley (SO 705 475; SO 74 NW 6)

Suckley Court (SO 713 513; SO 75 SW 4)

Whitbourne (SO 726 568; SO 75 NW 1)

Wells

The following is a selective list of some of the more historically significant springs, spouts, fountains and wells. Weaver and Osborne (1994) list about sixty and there are probably many more.

Cattern's (St Catherine's) Well (SO 793 529; SO 75 SE 7)

Chalybeate Spring (SO 777 457; (Weaver and Osborne 1994, 152–6))

Ditchford's Well (SO 769 406; SO 74 SE 11)

Eye Well★ (SO 769 423; SO 74 SE 9)

Eye Well (SO 744 526; SO 75 SW 10)

Hay Well★ (SO 775 457; (Weaver and Osborne 1994, 135–9))

Holy Well★ (SO 770 423; SO 74 SE 10)

Morarl's Well★ (SO 766 425; (Goodbury 1999, AX))

Pewtress Well (SO 760 403; SO 74 SE 4)

Primes Well (SO 768 436 (location uncertain); (Goodbury 1999, AA))

St Ann's Well★ (SO 772 457; SO 74NE 7)

St Thomas' Well★ (SO 768 442; (Goodbury 1999, AH))

Walm's Well★ (SO 760 392; SO 73 NE 7)

Appendix 2
The RCHME/EH Project

Throughout the 1980s and 1990s the Royal Commission on the Historical Monuments of England (RCHME – now part of English Heritage) undertook a considerable amount of collaborative work with National Park Authorities (Taylor 1991) in order to enhance understanding of the archaeological landscapes under the management of these bodies and to promote its future conservation. The fruits of this work have now been seen in a number of publications (eg Bowden 2000b; Riley and Wilson-North 2001). By 1998 it was felt that the time had come to launch an initiative to work with a different tier of conservation authorities – the Areas of Outstanding Natural Beauty (AONB). The Malvern Hills AONB, at 105 square kilometres, is one of the smaller AONBs and therefore was felt to be suitable for a pilot study. Following informal discussions between the RCHME and David Hancock, the then AONB Officer, the AONB's Joint Advisory Committee (JAC) requested a 'comprehensive archaeological survey of the Malvern Hills AONB'. They asked the RCHME to consider two tasks: detailed surveys of the six Scheduled Ancient Monuments (SAMs) that lie within the AONB; and a survey of the entire AONB landscape identifying, recording and interpreting the archaeological evidence, to act as a guide for future management.

The RCHME acceded to this request readily because, as noted above, it had a general policy interest in involvement with conservation-related work in partnership with landscape managers. More specifically, it assisted in the formulation of a positive response to the Countryside Commission's recent publication *Protecting Our Finest Countryside: Advice to Government*. A project on the Malvern Hills would help to assess effective means, in the context of AONBs, of securing 'a reliable record of the extent and state of the cultural resource' of archaeological remains and could contribute to the second objective of 'developing further more complete benchmarks for the satisfactory management of the cultural heritage' (Countryside Commission 1998, 21–2). The project was visualised as forming the first phase of a larger enterprise, the second phase of which, a Management Action and Monitoring Programme, would be undertaken by the relevant local authority Archaeological Officers.

As part of the partnership agreement the AONB Officer secured financial contributions towards the costs of the project from a wide range of interested bodies including local authorities, the Council for the Protection of Rural England (CPRE), the Malvern Hills Conservators (MHC) and the National Trust (NT). This income was targeted specifically towards the non-staff costs of large-scale survey, to bringing forward air photographic transcription of the area as a priority and to underpinning the costs of background documentary research.

Methodology

The project consisted of two distinct parts, as defined by the JAC's request: detailed survey of the SAMs and landscape survey.

Large-scale analytical survey
The first part was preceded by field reconnaissance. As a result of this it was decided that not all the SAMs would benefit from large-scale analytical earthwork survey. British Camp, Midsummer Hill and Bronsil Castle, however, were all surveyed at 1:1000 and subject to detailed Level 3 reports while the Shire Ditch and the cairns on Pinnacle Hill were studied at Level 2 (*see* RCHME 1999 or Bowden 1999, Appendix 1 for a description of 'Levels of Survey'). All survey was undertaken by the EH Archaeological

Investigation team using standard RCHME methods involving both electronic and traditional techniques (Bowden 1999, chapters 4 and 5; EH 2002).

The second part required a number of distinct tasks involving aerial and field archaeology, and documentary research. This part of the project was not restricted to the boundary of the AONB but took in the whole of the eleven Ordnance Survey 1:10 000 scale map sheets which cover the area (see Fig 1.8). The project did not include any excavation or other intrusive activities, though a small excavation at Cradley by Herefordshire Archaeology (Hoverd 2000b) was carried out simultaneously.

Aerial survey
by Helen Winton
The aerial survey of the Malvern Hills AONB comprised two parts: aerial reconnaissance, and mapping from aerial photographs. The mapping forms part of a major English Heritage (formerly RCHME) project, The National Mapping Programme (NMP), which aims to map all archaeology visible on aerial photographs in England (Bewley 2001). The aerial survey of the Malverns covered 275 square kilometres, which incorporates the AONB itself and a wider contextual area (as noted above).

The aerial reconnaissance was carried out in collaboration with the Archaeological Investigation team and the NMP team to target known archaeological features in the vicinity of the AONB and to look for new sites. Five sorties were carried out during the summer and winter of 1999 and 2000 at appropriate times for cropmark and earthwork photography (Wilson 2000, 38–87). The EH (formerly RCHME) Aerial Reconnaissance team consists of an aerial surveyor and a pilot, who use a high-winged light aircraft – a Cessna 172. Landscape views and well-known sites were photographed as well as a number of previously unrecognised earthwork and cropmark sites, in particular around the southern end of the AONB boundary.

Interpretation and mapping were carried out for any archaeological features, potentially dating from the Neolithic period to the 20th century, which show on aerial photographs as cropmarks, soilmarks, earthworks or structures. The main source for the NMP survey was the specialist

oblique and vertical collections of aerial photographs held at the National Monuments Record (NMR) and the Unit for Landscape Modelling at Cambridge (formerly Cambridge University Committee for Aerial Photography), supplemented by photography from the relevant county councils and the MHC. The specialist oblique photographs, especially from the recent reconnaissance, are site specific and tend to date from the last twenty years. These most notably include the work of Chris Musson, Harold Wingham and Arnold Baker. The vertical photographs provide almost blanket coverage of the area and were taken at regular intervals from 1942 to the present. The majority were taken by the RAF for training purposes and by the OS for mapping. Additional photography was sourced from commercial companies, such as Meridian Surveys. The vertical photographs give an essential historical perspective, with information on many sites that have been ploughed level or removed in the last fifty years.

The mapping was carried out in an entirely digital environment so that information contained on numerous photographs can be interpreted and combined to provide an overview of the archaeology over a large area. Each archaeological 'monument' was interpreted, described and recorded in the NMR database. All the photographs, maps, monument records and a report synthesising the main findings of the aerial survey (Winton 2004) are available from the NMR.

Documentary research
Owing to the financial partnership arrangements mentioned above, it was possible to obtain the services of Valerie Goodbury, a historian with extensive local knowledge, to undertake documentary research on behalf of the project. This resulted in a report (Goodbury 1999) and a set of annotated maps early in the progress of the project, which proved of inestimable value to the project team.

Landscape survey
The completed aerial transcription sheets and information from the documentary research were taken into the field by Investigators for selective evaluation. Unfortunately this phase of activity was

interrupted by the foot-and-mouth outbreak of 2001, leading to a serious curtailment of activity and delay in the completion of the project. Each map sheet was walked and a Level 1 investigation carried out. Changes to visible archaeological features since the date of the aerial photography were noted and previously unrecorded sites added. Time restrictions meant that complete coverage was not possible but approximately 30% of the area was investigated. It was intended at the outset that the most interesting sites located through aerial, documentary and field research would be surveyed analytically at large scale, but again the time restrictions, exacerbated by the foot-and-mouth outbreak, restricted this activity severely.

Woodland survey

Woodland, which is of course not susceptible to aerial survey, was treated as a separate entity for the purposes of the project. At an early stage it was decided that survey of the woodlands would be undertaken by the relevant local authority archaeologists as their distinct contribution to the project. As with the landscape survey, total coverage within the time available was impossible, so a sampling strategy was adopted, with archaeologists and voluntary helpers walking transects through blocks of woodland, noting features of archaeological interest. Hand-held navigational GPS (Global Positioning by Satellite) was used to locate features on the map at small scale.

Results of the project

The first product of the project is an enhanced National Monuments Record and local Sites and Monuments Record database for the area, informing better management and conservation through the Management Action and Monitoring Programme. Another outcome will be the promotion of further archaeological research to address some of the questions raised by the project (*see* Chapter 4).

References

Alcock, L 1965 'Hillforts in Wales and the Marches'. *Antiquity* **39**, 184–95

Allen, D F 1967 'Iron currency bars in Britain'. *Proc Prehist Soc* **33**, 307–35

Allen Brown, R 1989 *Castles, Conquest and Charters: collected papers.* Woodbridge: Boydell Press

Allies, J 1852 *On the Ancient British, Roman and Saxon Antiquities and Folklore of Worcestershire* (2 edn). London: J H Parker

Anon 1900 'The Gullet Pass, Ragged Stone Hill and Chase End Hill, the southern end of the Malverns'. *Trans Woolhope Natur Field Club* [15] (1898), 58–62

Ashmore, A and Knapp, A B (eds) 1999 *Archaeologies of Landscape.* Oxford: Blackwell

Aston, M 1993 *Monasteries.* London: B T Batsford

Bassett, S 2000 'How the west was won: the Anglo-Saxon takeover of the west midlands'. *Anglo-Saxon Studies in Archaeol and History* **11**, 107–18

Bewley, R H 2001 'Understanding England's historic landscapes: an aerial perspective'. *Landscapes* **2.1**, 74–78

BGS 1988 *1:50 000 Series map Sheet 216 – Tewkesbury.* Nottingham

— 1993 *1:50 000 Series Map Sheet 199 – Worcester.* Nottingham

Blake, J E H 1913 'Some remains of the Bronze Age at Mathon'. *Trans Birmingham Archaeol Soc.* **39** (1914), 90–3

— 1914 'Note on remains of the Bronze Age in Worcestershire'. *Trans Birmingham Archaeol Soc* **40** (1915), 83

Bond, C J 1978 'Moated sites in Worcestershire', *in* Aberg, F A (ed) *Medieval Moated Sites.* CBA Res Rep **17**, 71–7

— 1981 'The marshlands of Malvern Chase', *in* Rowley, R T (ed) *The Evolution of Marshland Landscapes.* Oxford: Oxford University Dept for External Stud, 95–112

— 1988 'Church and parish in Norman Worcestershire', *in* Blair, J (ed) *Minsters and Parish Churches: the local church in transition 950–1200.* Oxford: Oxford Univ Comm Archaeol Monogr **17**, 119–58

Bowden, M C B 2000a *British Camp or Herefordshire Beacon.* Swindon: EH Archaeol Investig Rep AI/4/2000

— 2002 *Berrow Hill, Martley, Worcestershire: level 2 archaeological survey.* Swindon: EH Archaeol Investig Rep AI/32/2002

— (ed) 1999 *Unravelling the Landscape: an inquisitive approach to archaeology.* Stroud: Tempus/RCHME

— (ed) 2000b *Furness Iron: the physical remains of the iron industry and associated woodland industries of Furness and southern Lakeland.* Swindon: English Heritage

Bowen, A R 1949 'Considerations on certain flint implements and other antiquities from the Worcester and Malvern district'. *Trans Worcestershire Archaeol Soc* **26**, 32–7

Bradley, R J 2000 *An Archaeology of Natural Places.* London: Routledge

Brown, A E 1961 'Records of surface finds made in Herefordshire, 1951–60'. *Trans Woolhope Natur Field Club* **37**, 77–91

Buckland, P C, Parker Pearson, M, Wigley, A and Girling, M A 2001 'Is there anybody out there? A reconsideration of the environmental evidence from the Breiddin hillfort, Powys, Wales'. *Antiq J* **81**, 51–76

Calloway, C 1900 'Notes on the origins of the gneisses and schists of the Malvern Hills'. *Trans Woolhope Natur Field Club* [15] (1898–9), 67–8

Conder, E 1898 'The geology of the Colwall district, with notes on the discovery of brine'. *Trans Woolhope Natur Field Club* [14] (1895–7), 212–14

Cope, J C W, Ingham, J K and Rawson, P F (eds) 1992 *Atlas of Palaeogeography and Lithofacies.* London: Geological Society, Memoir **13**

Coulson, C 1979 'Structural symbolism in medieval castle architecture'. *J Brit Archaeol Assoc* **132**, 73–90

Cunliffe, B W 1991 *Iron Age Communities in Britain* (3 edn). London: Routledge

Darvill, T 1989 'The circulation of Neolithic stone and flint axes: a case study from Wales and the mid-west of England'. *Proc Prehist Soc* **55**, 27–44

Dreghorn, W 1967 *Geology Explained in the Severn Vale and Cotswolds.* Newton Abbott: David & Charles.

Duff, P McL D and Smith, A J (eds) 1992 *Geology of England and Wales.* London: Geological Society

Dyer, C 1990 'Dispersed settlements in medieval England: a case study of Pendock, Worcestershire'. *Medieval Archaeol* **34**, 97–121

Eagles, B N 2001 'Anglo-Saxon presence and culture in Wiltshire *c* AD 450–*c* 675', *in* Ellis, P (ed) *Roman Wiltshire and After.* Devizes: Wiltshire Archaeol Natur Hist Soc

Earp, J R and Haines, B A 1971 *The Welsh Borderland* (3 edn). NERC/IGS Regional Geology. London: HMSO

EH 2002 *With Alidade and Tape: graphical and plane table survey of archaeological earthworks.* Swindon: English Heritage

Ekwall, E 1960 *Concise Oxford Dictionary of English Place Names* (4 edn). Oxford: Oxford Univ P

Everson, P L 1998 ' "Delightfully surrounded with woods and ponds": field evidence for medieval gardens in England', *in* Pattison, P (ed) *There by Design: field archaeology in parks and gardens.* Oxford: RCHME/Archaeopress, 32–8

Everson, P L and Jecock, M 1999 'Castle Hill and the early medieval development of Thetford in Norfolk', *in* Pattison, P, Field, D and Ainsworth, S (eds) *Patterns of the Past.* Oxford: Oxbow, 97–106

Field, D 2000 *Midsummer Hill Camp: a survey of the earthworks on Midsummer and Hollybush Hills, Eastnor.* Swindon: EH Archaeol Investig Rep AI/16/2000

Finberg, H P R 1975 *The Gloucestershire Landscape.* London: Hodder & Stoughton

Gelling, M 1978 *Signposts to the Past: place-names and the history of England.* London: Dent

— 1992 *The West Midlands in the Early Middle Ages.* Leicester: Leicester Univ P

Gent, H 1983 'Centralised storage in later prehistoric Britain'. *Proc Prehist Soc* **49**, 243–68

Goodbury, V 1999 'Documentary Research'. Typescript report for the archaeological survey of the Malvern Hills AONB by English Heritage (formerly RCHME)

Greene, J P 1992 *Medieval Monasteries*. Leicester: Leicester Univ P

Griffin, S, Jackson, R, Jones, L and Pearson, E 2000 *Evaluation of land at DERA, Malvern, Worcestershire*. Worcester: WCC Archaeological Service Rep **859**

Grubb, T and Derham, K 2003 *Malvern Hills AONB Survey – Bromsberrow Place*. GCC Archaeology Service

Hamilton, W G 1940 'A Bronze Age burial site at Southend, Mathon', *Trans Woolhope Natur Field Club* **29** (1936–8), 120–7

Higham, R and Barker, P 1992 *Timber Castles*. London: B T Batsford

Hill, J D 1996 'Hillforts and the Iron Age of Wessex', *in* Champion, T C and Collis, J R (eds) *The Iron Age in Britain and Ireland: recent trends*. Sheffield: J R Collis Publs, 95–116

Hillaby, J G 1997 *Ledbury: a Medieval Borough* (2 edn). Woonton Almeley: Ledbury & Dist Soc Trust/Logaston Press

Hilton Price, F G 1887 'Camps on the Malvern Hills', *Trans Woolhope Natur Field Club* **[9]** (1877–80), 217–28

Hingley, R 1990 'Iron Age "currency bars": the archaeological and social context', *Archaeol J* **147**, 91–117

Hirsch, E and O'Hanlon, M (eds) 1995 *The Anthropology of Landscape*. Oxford: Clarendon Press

Hooke, D 1985 *The Anglo-Saxon Landscape: the Kingdom of the Hwicce*. Manchester: Manchester Univ P
— 1990 *Worcestershire Anglo-Saxon Charter Bounds*. London: Boydell Press

Hoverd, T 2000a 'Ledbury, woodland survey'. *West Midlands Archaeol* **43**, 47–8
— 2000b 'Ridgeway, Cradley: an Iron Age enclosure', *West Midlands Archaeol* **43**, 45–6
— 2003 *The Archaeological Survey of Herefordshire Woodlands in the Malvern Hills AONB, 1999–2003*. Herefordshire Archaeol: Herefordshire Archaeol Rep **101**

Hughes, I T 1926 'Report on the excavations conducted on Midsummer Hill Camp', *Trans Woolhope Natur Field Club* **[23]** (1924–6), 18–27

Hurle, P 1978 *Hanley Castle: heart of Malvern Chase*. Chichester: Phillimore

Jack, G H 1914a 'Some notes on Roman Herefordshire', *Trans Woolhope Natur Field Club* **[19]** (1908–11), 68–73
— 1914b 'Roman road between Monmouth and Gloucester, with a note on the Roman masonry at Donnington', *Trans Woolhope Natur Field Club* **[19]** (1908–11), 105–9

Jackson, D 1999 'Variation in size distribution of hillforts in the Welsh Marches and its implication for social organization', *in* Bevan: B (ed) *Northern Exposure: interpretative devolution and the Iron Ages of Britain*. Leicester: Leicester Archaeol Monogr **4**, 197–216

King, D J C and Alcock, L 1969 'Ringworks of England and Wales', *Chateau Gaillard* **3**, 90–127

Leech, R 1981 *Historic Towns in Gloucestershire*. Bristol: CRAAGS

Lewis, S G and Maddy, D (eds) 1997 *The Quaternary of the South Midlands and the Welsh Marches: Field Guide*. London: Quat Res Ass

Lines, H H nd *The Ancient Camps on the Malvern Hills*. Worcester: Phillips & Probert

Maddy, D 1997 'Midlands drainage development', *in* Lewis, S G and Maddy, D (eds) 1997, 7–18

McOmish, D S, Field, D and Brown, G 2002 *The Field Archaeology of the Salisbury Plain Training Area*. London: English Heritage

McWhirr, A 1981 *Roman Gloucestershire*. Gloucester: Alan Sutton

Millett, M 1990 *The Romanization of Britain: an essay in archaeological interpretation*. Cambridge: Cambridge Univ P

Mindykowski, A and Bretherton, J 2003 *Malvern Hills Woodland Archaeology: results of recent survey in Worcestershire*. WCC Historic Environment and Archaeology Service

Moore, H C 1896 'Flint flakes'. *Trans Woolhope Natur Field Club* **[13]** (1893–4), 191–3

Moore, T forthcoming a 'The early to later Iron Age transition in the Severn–Cotswolds'
— forthcoming b 'Life on the edge? Exchange, community and identity in the later Iron Age of the Severn–Cotswolds'

O'Kelly, M 1982 *Newgrange*. London: Thames & Hudson

Peacock, D P S 1967 'Romano-British pottery production in the Malvern district, Worcestershire', *Trans Worcestershire Archaeol Soc* 3 ser **1** (1965–7), 15–28
— 1968 'A petrological study of certain Iron Age pottery from western England', *Proc Prehist Soc* **34**, 414–27

Piggott, S 1938 'The Early Bronze Age in Wessex', *Proc Prehist Soc* **4**, 52–106

Piper, G H 1898 'The camp and ancient British town on the Midsummer and Hollybush Hills of the Malvern range', *Trans Woolhope Field Club* **[15]** (1898–9), 69–71

Rahtz, P and Watts, L 2003 *Glastonbury: myth and archaeology* (2 edn). Stroud: Tempus

RCHME 1932 *An Inventory of the Historical Monuments in Herefordshire 2 – East*. London: HMSO
— 1999 *Recording Archaeological Field Monuments: a descriptive specification*. Swindon: RCHME

Richards, A E 1997 'Middle Pleistocene deposits in north-east Herefordshire', *in* Lewis, S G and Maddy, D (eds) 1997, 75–88

Riley, H and Wilson-North, R 2001 *The Field Archaeology of Exmoor*. Swindon: English Heritage

Roberts, B K and Wrathmell, S 2002 *Region and Place: a study of English rural settlement*. London: English Heritage

Robertson, A S 2000 *An Inventory of Romano-British Coin Hoards*. Roy Numis Soc Spec Publ **20**

Robinson, S F G 1971 'Two flint arrowheads from the Ledbury area', *Herefordshire Archaeol News* **22**, 2

Sawle, J 1981 'Whitbourne, Hereford and Worcester: excavations at hill-fort', *West Midlands Archaeol* **24**, 130

Sherratt, A 1996 'Why Wessex? The Avon route and river transport in later British prehistory', *Oxford J Archaeol* **15**(2), 211–34

Smith, B S 1978 *A History of Malvern* (2 edn). Stroud: Alan Sutton/The Malvern Bookshop

Smith, C N S 1957 'A catalogue of the prehistoric finds from Worcestershire', *Trans Worcestershire Archaeol Soc* **34**, 1–27

Smith, N A 2001 *Bronsil Castle, Eastnor, Herefordshire: a survey of the remains of a 15th-century mansion, its surrounding moat, and ponds*. Swindon: EH Archaeol Investig Rep AI/14/2001

Smith, R A 1905 'On the ancient British iron currency', *Proc Soc Antiqs* **20**, 179–95

Soil Survey 1983 *Soil Map of England and Wales*. Harpenden: Soil Survey

Stanford, S C 1980 *The Archaeology of the Welsh Marches*. London: Collins
— 1981 *Midsummer Hill: an Iron Age Hillfort on the Malverns*. Hereford: printed privately
— 1988 *The Malvern Hillforts: Midsummer Hill and British Camp*. Great Malvern: Malvern Hills Conservators

Swan, V G 1984 *The Pottery Kilns of Roman Britain*. RCHME Supplementary Series **5**. London: HMSO

Taylor, C C 1991 'Archaeological field survey in the National Parks by the Royal Commission on the Historical Monuments of England', *in* White, R F and Iles, R (eds) *Archaeology in National Parks*. Bainbridge: National Parks Staff Assoc/Yorkshire Dales National Park, 65–8

Thomas, G N 1997 'Pleistocene vegetation history of the English Midlands', *in* Lewis, S G and Maddy, D (eds) 1997, 19–30

Toomey, J P 2001 *Records of Hanley Castle, Worcestershire,* c *1147–1547*. Worcestershire Hist Soc ns **18**

VCR Worcesteershire 1924 *The Victoria County History of the County of Worcestershire* **4**. London: St Catherine Press

Waters, P L 1963 'A Romano-British tile kiln at Upper Sandlin Farm, Leigh Sinton, Worcestershire', *Trans Worcestershire Archaeol Soc* **40**, 1–5

— 1976 'Romano-British pottery site at Great Buckmans Farm', *Trans Worcestershire Archaeol Soc* 3 ser **5**., 63–72

Watkins, A 1932 'Romano-British pottery in Herefordshire', *Trans Woolhope Natur Field Club* (1930–2), 110–12

Watt, S (ed) forthcoming *West Midlands Archaeological Research Framework*. London: English Heritage

Weaver, C 1998 'From private pursuit to public playground: the enclosure of Malvern Chase', *Trans Worcestershire Archaeol Soc* 3 ser **16**, 207–19

Weaver, C and Osborne, B 1994 *Aquae Malvernensis: a history and topography of the springs, spouts, fountains and wells of the Malverns and the development of a public water supply*. Malvern: Cora Weaver

Webster, G 1954 'A trial trench across the defences of the Roman fort at Tedstone Wafre', *Trans Woolhope Natur Field Club* **34** (1955), 284–92

Webster, P V 1976 'Severn Valley Ware: a preliminary study', *Trans Bristol Gloucestershire Archaeol Soc* **94**, 18–46

Wheeler, R E M 1953 'The Herefordshire Beacon hillfort', *Archaeol J* **109** (1952), 146–8

Williams, P 1979 *Whitbourne: a bishop's manor*. Whitbourne: Hamish Park

Wilson D R 2000 *Air Photo Interpretation for Archaeologists* (2 edn). Stroud: Tempus

Winton, H 2004 *Malvern Hills AONB National Mapping Programme Project Report*. Swindon: English Heritage

Woodcock, N H and Strachan, R A (eds) 2000 *Geological history of Britain and Ireland*. Oxford: Blackwell Science

Wootton, D and Bowden, M C B 2002 *A circular enclosure at Redmarley d'Abitot, Gloucestershire*. Swindon: EH Archaeol Investig Rep AI/43/2002

Wymer, J J 1996 *The English Rivers Palaeolithic Project 1994–5: the Thames Valley and Warwickshire Avon, Report 1*. London: English Heritage/Trust for Wessex Archaeol

Wymer, J J with Bonsall, C J 1977 *Gazetteer of Mesolithic Sites in England and Wales with a Gazetteer of Upper Palaeolithic Sites in England and Wales*. (Counc Brit Archaeol Res Rep **20**) London: Counc Brit Archaeol

Index